ANIMAL RIGHTS

yes or no?

Marna Owen

LERNER PUBLICATIONS COMPANY • MINNEAPOLIS

Library of Congress Cataloging-in-Publication Data

Owen, Marna A.
    Animal rights—yes or no? / by Marna A. Owen.
        p.   cm. — (Pro/Con)
    Includes bibliographical references (p.   ) and index.
    Summary: Examines the treatment of animals in such areas as medical research, agriculture, fashion, and industry and explores opposing viewpoints on the question of whether animals have rights.
    ISBN 0-8225-2603-4
    1. Animal rights—Juvenile literature. 2. Animal rights—United States—Juvenile literature. [1. Animal rights. 2. Animals—Treatment.] I. Title. II. Series
HV4708.O84   1992
179'.3—dc20   91-38515
                                                                CIP
                                                                 AC

Manufactured in the United States of America

1 2 3 4 5 6 – P/JR – 98 97 96 95 94 93

CONTENTS

FOREWORD

If a nation expects to be ignorant and free,...it expects what never was and never will be.   —*Thomas Jefferson*

Are you ready to participate in forming the policies of our government? Many issues are very confusing, and it can be difficult to know what to think about them or how to make a decision about them. Sometimes you must gather information about a subject before you can be informed enough to make a decision. Bernard Baruch, a prosperous American financier and an advisor to every president from Woodrow Wilson to Dwight D. Eisenhower, said, "If you can get all the facts, your judgment can be right; if you don't get all the facts, it can't be right."

But gathering information is only one part of the decision-making process. The way you interpret information is influenced by the values you have been taught since, infancy—ideas about right and wrong, good and bad. Many of your values are shaped, or at least influenced, by how and where you grow up, by your race, sex, and religion, by how much money your family has. What your parents believe, what they read, and what you read and believe influence your decisions. The values of friends and teachers also affect what you think.

It's always good to listen to the opinions of people around you, but you will often confront contradictory points of view and points of view that are based not on fact, but on myth. John F Kennedy, the 35th president of the United States, said, "The great enemy of the truth is very often not the lie-deliberate, contrived, and dishonest-

4

but the myth-persistent, persuasive, and unrealistic." Eventually, you will have to separate fact from myth and make up your own mind, make your own decisions. Because you are responsible for your decisions, it's important to get as much information as you can. Then your decisions will be the right ones for you.

Making a fair and informed decision can be an exciting process, a chance to examine new ideas and different points of view. You live in a world that changes quickly and sometimes dramatically-a world that offers the opportunity to explore the ever-changing ground between yourself and others. Instead of forming a single, easy, or popular point of view, you might develop a rich and complex vision that offers new alternatives. Explore the many dimensions of an idea. Find kinship among an extensive range of opinions. Only after you've done this should you try to form your own opinions.

After you have formed an opinion about a particular subject, you may believe it is the only right decision. But some people will disagree with you and challenge your beliefs. They are not trying to antagonize you or put you down. They probably believe that they're right as sincerely as you believe you are. Thomas Macaulay, an English historian and author, wrote, "Men are never so likely to settle a questions rightly as when they discuss it freely." In a democracy, the free exchange of ideas is not only encouraged, it's vital. Examining and discussing public issues and understanding opposing ideas are desirable and necessary elements of a free nation's ability to govern itself.

This Pro/Con series is designed to explore and examine different points of view on contemporary issues and to help you develop an understanding and appreciation of them. Most importantly, it will help you form your own opinions and make your own honest, informed decisions.

Mary Winget
Series Editor

Before the Salk vaccine was developed, the iron lung, right, *was both a prison and a link to life for polio victims. Dr. Jonas E. Salk vaccinates a child as a nurse assists,* below.

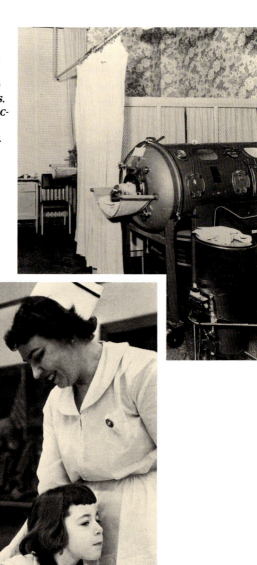

THE DEBATE

Although April 24, 1990, was a warm spring day, an unusual tension spread across the campus of the University of California, Berkeley. Amidst the blooming flowers and singing birds, hundreds of students, scientists, and community members gathered to voice their views on a tough question: Should animals be used in medical research?

During a press conference, the Coalition for Animals and Animal Research (CFAAR) answered the question with a resolute "yes." To make their point, CFAAR members wheeled in an iron lung, a cylinder approximately seven feet long and three feet wide that allows people with paralyzed chest muscles to breathe. Professor Charles Niccol, a university scientist, explained that poliomyelitis, commonly known as polio, once infected thousands of people each year. The virus caused paralysis (loss of muscle control), an inability to breathe, and sometimes death. In the United States, most cases occurred in children between 4 and 15 years old.

Niccol and other CFAAR members told reporters that they were celebrating the 35th anniversary of the Salk polio vaccine, developed by Jonas E. Salk. Because of this vaccine, first used in 1955, polio can now be prevented. Niccol pointed out that the vaccine could never have been developed without the aid of tens of thousands of monkeys that were injected with the polio virus. By using their infected tissue, Dr. Salk was able to develop a vaccine that would prevent infection.

Niccol reminded reporters that there are still many more people to be saved. Cancer, Alzheimer's disease, and AIDS are only a few of the terrible diseases that still cause human suffering and death. With the help of animal research, these diseases might also be conquered. What better argument can there be for continuing the use of animals in research?[1]

THE FIERY REPLY

While Niccol spoke, animal rights supporters began to make their own case on Berkeley's Sproul Plaza. They organized a protest march as a grand finale to World Laboratory Animal Liberation Week. Protesters waved pictures of monkeys used in laboratory experiments and signs reading "Stop the Testing and the Torture," as they held up a mock figure of a research scientist. Wrapped in a white lab coat with red dollar signs painted on the collar, the figure was meant to symbolize the money spent each year for research animals. As the activists chanted, they burned the figure in effigy. They claimed that each year 80,000 animals are used—and often killed—for the sake of medical research. They also described experiments in which puppies are burned, cats' eyelids are sewn shut, and baboons' heads are crushed. The protesters then questioned whether such acts can be justified.

Tempers flared as insults and arguments shot back and forth between the CFAAR members and the animal rights groups. A half-dozen protesters chained themselves to a fence outside the psychology building, where animals are used in research. Another group threw stones through the windows of the Northwest Animal Facility, Berkeley's new $14 million animal research lab. In the end, police arrested 28 protesters, but nothing was resolved.[2]

THE CONTROVERSY
This incident represents two sides of a complicated debate, one that goes far beyond the use of animals in medical research. It is a controversy that raises many questions about how we use animals in our daily lives.

For example, should humans eat meat? Many animal rights groups believe that we systematically "murder" billions of cows, pigs, and chickens each year for food. While some animal rights supporters argue for strict vegetarianism (meatless diets), others want laws that enforce painless methods of butchering the animals.

Many people reply that by eating meat, humans are simply carrying out their natural role in the food chain. Animals eat plants or other animals; so do humans. Why is the practice of cats eating birds and mice thought to be natural, while the practice of humans eating meat, fish, or poultry is thought to be wrong, or at least questionable?

Should humans use animals for clothing? The practice dates back to the earliest humans, who used the skins of other species for clothing. Some animal rights advocates argue that technology has provided us with synthetic (artificial) materials that can be used in place of animal skins. But many other people argue that nothing matches the beauty, quality, and durability of products made from natural skins. They also point out that many synthetic materials

In general, monkeys crave social contact. Above, *two research monkeys touch after a long period of isolation.*

are made from chemical processes that pollute the environment.

Should humans keep other animal species as pets, or is the very word *pet* demeaning? Some activists favor the term *companion animal* and believe that house animals deserve the same treatment as family members and friends.[3] But do nonhuman animals actually have the same rights as humans, and do they deserve the same treatment?

Most people in the world do not advocate cruelty to animals. But these same people may wonder why they should be as concerned about animals as they are about humans. Many react negatively to the extreme, sometimes illegal, tactics used by some activists. Most people probably seek a middle ground that protects animals but allows them to be used, without cruelty, for specific purposes, such as food, clothing, and medical research.

A group of activists protest the use of lab animals at New York University.

This book examines our relationships with and responsibilities toward animals. At the heart of the animal rights debate are these questions: Do all animals have rights just as humans do? Do humans have the right to use other species for their own purposes? Is there some middle ground on which the two sides can agree?

The remaining chapters in this book take a look at both sides of the animal rights debate. And, as with most issues, there seem to be almost as many opinions as there are people.

The ancient Greek philosopher Aristotle thought human beings had dominion over animals.

THE QUESTION
OF RIGHTS

To have a right is to have a claim or entitlement to something and to have that claim recognized by others. In all societies, humans are believed to have certain rights—both legal (such as the right to vote) and moral. Moral rights, often called human rights, are more difficult to define than legal rights. They include such entitlements as "life, liberty, and the pursuit of happiness," as referred to in the Declaration of Independence.

Humans believe that their moral rights stem from such qualities as reason, language, sentience (the ability to feel), self-awareness, forethought, intrinsic value (worth), and a sense of personal identity. Should rights for animals be based on the same criteria? For thousands of years, philosophers have wrestled with the question of animal rights: Do animals have rights? Are humans superior to other animals on earth? Can animals reason, feel, and communicate?

AN ANCIENT DEBATE
Hinduism, the major religion of India, is one of the oldest religions in the world. Its roots reach back to prehistoric times.

According to Hindu beliefs, animals have immortal souls just as human beings do. Hindus worship many animals as gods. Cows are the most sacred, but Hindus also worship monkeys, snakes, and other animals. Hinduism teaches that the soul never dies. When the body dies, the soul is reborn. In this continuous process of rebirth, called reincarnation, the soul can be reborn in an animal or in a human. Because of their beliefs, Hindus practice vegetarianism.

European societies, on the other hand, have long believed in human superiority over animals. The ancient Greek philosopher Aristotle (384–322 B.C.) saw humans as rational animals, animals that could reason. Because humans can reason, Aristotle thought, they rightly had dominion, or power, over plants and animals. He wrote that in the natural order of things, plants live to provide food for animals. In turn, animals live to supply humans with food, clothing, and tools. According to Aristotle, humans were just fulfilling their part in the natural hierarchy by using and consuming animals.[1]

Christianity, the religion of much of Europe and the Americas, is rooted in the belief that humans are superior to animals. The story of creation puts forth a clear statement about the relationship between humans and other animals. In the book of Genesis (1:26), the Bible states:

> And God said, Let us make man in our image, after our likeness: and let them have dominion over the fish of the sea, and over the fowl of the air, and over the earth, and over every creeping thing that creepeth upon the earth.

The Bible denies equal rights to animals. It implies that humans are superior beings with a special position in the

René Descartes was a 17th-century philosopher who thought that humans were superior to all other living things.

universe because they resemble God. The words in Genesis also say that humans have dominion over everything else on earth. Many people interpret this passage as God's permission for humans to use animals as they wish.

Christian doctrine also states that humans are the only animals with immortal souls—and thus the opportunity for spiritual life after bodily death. This doctrine has been held as truth for many centuries.

During the 1600s and 1700s, a period called the Enlightenment or the Age of Reason, European philosophers emphasized the use of reason as the best method of gaining truth. They believed that human beings had a unique advantage over all other creatures because humans can reason. Animals, in contrast, were thought to be slaves of their emotions. When an animal is angry, it fights. People, the philosophers argued, could solve their problems

through the use of reason. Philosophers of the Enlightenment also noted that people, unlike animals, had a rational
will—the ability to make and carry out plans.

René Descartes, a 17th-century French philosopher, math-
ematician, and scientist, is called the father of modern
philosophy. Descartes was a Christian who believed that
because humans had immortal souls and a mind with
which to reason, they were superior to all other living
things. He believed that only humans had consciousness—
which was shown by their unique capacity for language.
Descartes believed that animals did not have minds, souls,
or consciousness. Animals, in his view, were nothing more
than machines, incapable of feeling.[2]

At about the same time, doctors and scientists became
curious about anatomy, the study of the body. To learn how
blood flowed, scientists nailed the paws of live dogs to
boards and cut the dogs open.[3]

Experimenting on live animals without anesthesia, which
did not exist at that time, seems cruel to us now. But one
positive outcome of the experiments is that scientists were
able to see how closely the bodies of animals resemble the
bodies of humans. This resemblance eventually caused
some change in human attitudes toward animals and more
humane treatment of them. For example, in the middle of
the 18th century, the French author and philosopher
Voltaire referred to the "barbarous custom of supporting
ourselves upon the flesh and blood of beings like ourselves," although he himself continued the practice of
eating meat.[4]

However, in 1780 the German philosopher Immanuel
Kant told his students at Königsberg University that "so far
as animals are concerned, we have no direct duties.

Animals are not self-conscious, and are there merely as a means to an end. That end is man."[5] Kant believed that the life of every human being had intrinsic worth and that only humans had a right to life.

At about the same time that Kant was lecturing, a British philosopher named Jeremy Bentham began to promote the idea of animal welfare. Questioning theories about the difference between humans and animals, he wrote:

> Is it the faculty of reason, or perhaps the faculty of discourse [that distinguishes humans from animals]? But a full-grown horse or dog is beyond comparison a more rational, as well as a more conversable animal, than an infant of a day or week or even a month old. But suppose it were otherwise, what would it avail? The question is not, Can they *reason?* nor Can they *talk?* but, Can they *suffer?*[6]

Jeremy Bentham was one of the first people to promote the idea of animal welfare.

Many people take their pets to the annual "Blessing of the Animals" ceremony at St. John's Episcopal Church in New York.

Bentham believed that in deciding what is right and wrong, the suffering of *all* creatures—not just that of humans—should be taken into account.

Charles Darwin, an English naturalist, put forth a theory in the late 19th century that revolutionized the way humans looked at their place in the natural world. In 1859 Darwin published *On the Origin of Species.* In this book, Darwin proposed that one animal species could derive, or evolve, from another. Humans, however, were not yet included in Darwin's theory of evolution.

By 1871 many scientists had accepted Darwin's theory. In that year, he published *The Descent of Man,* a book that included humans in the evolutionary chain, stating that humans had evolved from other primates, such as apes and

In the 19th century, Charles Darwin revolutionized human thought when he introduced the theory of evolution. He is pictured here as a young man, as a middle aged man, and as an old man.

monkeys. Comparing the mental powers of humans and animals, he wrote:

> We have seen that the senses and intuitions, the various emotions and faculties, such as love, memory, attention and curiosity, imitation, reason, etc., of which man boasts, may be found in an incipient, or even sometimes in a well-developed condition, in the lower animals.[7]

Darwin went on to say that the human moral sense "can be traced back to social instincts in animals which lead them to take pleasure in each other's company, feel sympathy for each other, and perform services of mutual assistance."[8]

Darwin's book was extremely controversial, because it challenged the traditional relationship between humans and animals. His theory contradicted the words in Genesis. People had always viewed themselves as being superior to animals—as being a special creation of God. They did not want to think of themselves as being part of the animal world. Even now, some religious groups disagree with Darwin's theory that humans evolved from animals, although it is generally accepted by most scientists.

NEW DATA

The debate over animal rights and the relationship between humans and animals continues to this day. Are humans the only rational beings on earth?

Animal rights activists cite recent studies that show how animals use language. In the 1960s and 1970s, for example, scientists taught a number of primates to use sign language. While many of the animals could use signs only to ask for simple things like food and water, some could also combine signs in ways their teachers never showed them. One famous chimp named Lucy called a watermelon a "candy drink" and a radish a "hurt-cry food." A gorilla named Koko asked for a pet kitten and signed her sadness when it was killed.

Other studies in California and Hawaii show that some seals, sea lions, and dolphins can apply grammatical rules to language. For example, dolphins at the Kewalo Basin Marine Mammal Laboratory in Honolulu have been taught to understand about 50 words. According to lab director Lou Herman, the animals can carry out thousands of commands using only those 50 words. They understand the difference between "to left Frisbee, right surfboard take," and "to right surfboard, left Frisbee take." The sentences use the exact same words but have totally different meanings. Perhaps their understanding of such fine differences shows that these animals have higher reasoning abilities than was previously assumed.[9]

THE DEBATE CONTINUES

Many scientists and philosophers say that recent experiments prove only that some creatures, and very few indeed, can follow directions and have some limited capacity for language. They point out that dolphins do not write books, nor do chimpanzees build rockets to the moon. Humans, they say, are clearly the superior species on the planet.

Does this notion mean that humans can treat animals any way they want? Peter Singer, director of the Centre for Human Bioethics at Monash University, Australia, and the author of *Animal Liberation,* believes that because animals are sentient—can experience pain, suffering, enjoyment, and happiness—the pain of a rat is as important as the pain of a human. It is because animals are sentient, says Singer, that they deserve the same *consideration* given to humans. According to Singer, people who do not give equal consideration to animals make the same mistake as people who are racist or sexist. He calls these people *speciesists.*[10]

However, Singer points out that equal consideration for animals does not necessarily lead to equal rights and treatment. "There are important differences between humans and other animals," he explains, "and these differences must give rise to some differences in the rights that each have."[11]

When considering animal rights, Singer believes, people ought to think in terms of doing the greatest good for the greatest number of living things. We must weigh whether the good gained by using animals for certain purposes ex-

Scientists have proved that dolphins can apply grammatical rules to language. Does this mean they have the ability to reason?

ceeds the harm done to them. In other words, does the welfare of all outweigh the suffering of a few? Is a cure for cancer worth the lives of experimental animals?

Tom Regan, a contemporary American philosopher, rejects Singer's argument, which allows individual animals or humans to suffer if their suffering will benefit a great number of other humans or animals. Regan believes that all organisms have inherent value. Any organism that has beliefs, desires, perception, memory, a sense of the future, a sense of identity over time, and can be benefited or harmed ought to be treated in ways that respect its value. According to Regan, we fail to respect the inherent value of creatures when we do anything that harms them.

An organization called People for the Ethical Treatment of Animals (PETA) takes that philosophy a step further. PETA is a national, nonprofit animal protection organization founded by Alex Pacheo and Ingrid Newkirk. Its more than 250,000 members are dedicated to establishing what they perceive as the rights of animals. During a recent interview, Newkirk said that "animal liberationists do not separate out the human animal. A rat is a dog is a boy."[12] Newkirk's view is being expressed by a growing number of animal rights activists who believe that animals should not be used for food, clothing, or medical research. Modern technology, they argue, offers many alternatives to using animals.

SUMMARY

Current opinion about the rights of animals still runs a wide gamut, but it can generally be divided into three basic positions.

Sheep provide both food and clothing for humans. A growing number of people oppose the use of animals for such purposes.

Position 1: Humans are superior to animals. Animals are essentially our property, and we can use them as we please.

People who hold this position believe that we have dominion over animals. Many people scoff at the idea of giving animals any kind of rights. Rights, they say, by their very definition, are restricted to human beings. To some people, the idea of putting humans and pigs on equal footing seems absurd. For them, the suffering of a person with AIDS will always be more important than the suffering of a laboratory rat.

Position 2: Animals should be used only in ways that greatly benefit humankind. Whenever possible, these animals should be treated without cruelty.

People who hold this position, which includes many animal welfare groups, believe our responsibility is to treat animals with kindness. It is acceptable to use animals to accomplish goals that will benefit society, as long as we do so in the kindest way possible.

This position—the belief that animals should be treated humanely—is probably the most popular one held today. Most Americans eat some meat but prefer not to think about how animals are slaughtered to provide it. Most people would probably prefer livestock to be killed painlessly, and some might even work toward that end. News stories about lab rats used in cancer research are not upsetting to most people because they look beyond the potential suffering of the rats to the possibility of a cancer-free world. People treat their pets well, but few people see them as equals. Most people think kind treatment should be provided to animals, but not at the cost of human well-being. The bottom line for the majority of people who subscribe to the animal welfare position is that animals are important, but humans come first.

Position 3: Animals have basic rights just as humans do. Animals should be allowed to live their lives naturally and without cruelty. Humans do not have the right to dominate or exploit animals for any reason.

Animal rights activists see no significant differences between humans and animals. They believe that animals deserve treatment equal to that of human beings and that it is wrong for human beings to use animals in research and industry. They would like humans to allow animals to live their lives without interference.

Although opinion about the relationship between humans and animals has changed over the centuries, many questions remain unanswered. People's ideas about animals are influenced by many factors, such as religious beliefs, where they live, and the kind of work they do. Ranchers in the Southwest, for example, probably view cattle quite differently than do people who live in cities, where they may never encounter a cow except as packaged meat. To some people, pets are a messy nuisance; others treat them as human beings. A medical researcher may view rats as a means to cure disease; animal rights activists view the researcher's rats as helpless victims. Sometimes these various philosophies clash.

This young woman is protesting the use of driftnets, often used to catch tuna and salmon.

ANIMALS
AND THE LAW

In 1821, Alderman C. Smith suggested to the British Parliament that a law should be passed protecting horses from cruel treatment. The other members of Parliament snickered. "Next we'll have to protect dogs," yelled one. "And cats!" cried another. Soon the whole building shook with laughter at the thought. Protection for animals indeed! The notion was considered hilarious.[1]

Since then, attitudes about laws for the protection of animals have changed. Almost 170 years after the uproar in the British Parliament, the United Nations (U.N.) adopted a resolution calling for an end to all large-scale driftnet fishing by June 30, 1992. The fishing fleets of Japan, Taiwan, and Korea use driftnets, which are sometimes 50 miles long. They use the nets mainly to catch tuna, but dolphins, sea turtles, seals, and many other creatures get tangled and killed in them as well. Half a million seabirds die in the nets every year. Many of the animals that are caught cannot be sold, so they are thrown away. The U.N. resolution was passed to help stop the waste and to protect animal life.

This example shows how far animal protection laws have come. Once scoffed at, animal protection is now an international issue. While some groups say the laws have far to go, others say the laws have already gone too far. What are the most crucial laws affecting animals today?

LAWS FOR HUMANE SLAUGHTER

Before the 1800s, there was little organized effort to protect animals. In 1822 the British Parliament passed a bill that made the mistreatment of certain animals an offense. It was the first law of its kind, and it was very controversial. Under the new law, animals were viewed as property, not as beings worthy of rights. The law applied to work animals such as horses and donkeys—not to dogs and cats. And it was passed for the benefit of the owners, not the animals.

To enforce the new law, Richard Martin, a member of the British Parliament, and a group of other humanitarians formed the Royal Society for the Prevention of Cruelty to Animals in 1824. It was not until 1866 that Henry Bergh, a New York philanthropist, founded a similar organization, the American Society for the Prevention of Cruelty to Animals (ASPCA), in the United States.

The ASPCA began a crusade to provide animals with kinder, more humane treatment. One of the outcomes of this crusade was the 28-Hour Law. Passed in 1873, the law stated that animals transported to slaughterhouses by train had to be rested and given food and water every 28 hours. Before the law was passed, animals were sometimes jammed into railroad cars, where they suffered for days before they were butchered.[2]

In the early 1900s, many journalists took up the crusade for better laws to regulate the slaughter of animals. One of the most famous books of the time was *The Jungle*, written by Upton Sinclair. In his book, Sinclair described the unclean conditions of the Chicago slaughterhouses. Animals there were killed brutally. The blood of both diseased and healthy animals ran everywhere, infecting and spoiling meat headed for the marketplace.

As a result of this exposure, Congress passed the Pure Food and Drug Act in 1906. The act regulated health standards in slaughterhouses. Unfortunately, it also resulted in more hardship for the animals. The law stated that animals could not lie in each other's blood after being slaughtered. As a consequence, animals were suspended by one leg from a rope or chain and then axed to death. This practice ended in 1958 when Congress passed the Humane Slaughter Act. This law required that animals be stunned before being put to death.[3]

Do current slaughter laws adequately protect animals from unnecessary suffering? Some people might wonder what difference it makes, since the animals are about to die anyway. The strictest animal rights activists, however, say no. They would prefer that the slaughter of animals be outlawed. But, such a law would have a devastating effect on people involved in livestock production, such as farmers and ranchers, and those who work in the food industry.

Many animal welfare groups don't want to outlaw livestock production, but they tend to agree that the current laws are not adequate, and often they are not enforced. Typically, the animals are penned tightly while a worker stuns them, one by one, with an electric shock to their heads. Sometimes the shock is not strong enough, or its effect doesn't last until the animal is killed. An animal may become conscious while hoisted or before its throat is slit.

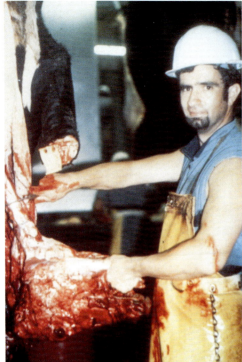

Meat packing is the business of slaughtering cattle, hogs, and sheep, and preparing the meat for transportation and sale.

At retail and wholesale establishments, butchers divide the meat into various cuts for consumers.

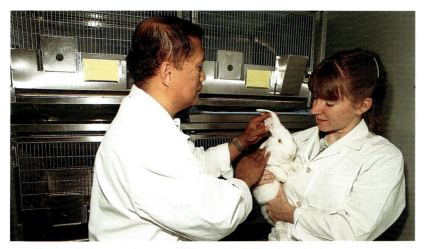

Researchers examine a rabbit used in laboratory tests.

Also, the Humane Slaughter Act applies only to slaughterhouses that sell meat to the federal government or its agencies. That means that 4,700 of the 6,100 slaughterhouses in the United States do not have to use stunning at all.[4] Animal welfare groups would like all creatures to be given the most humane treatment before slaughter. But up to now, strong lobbies representing farmers, ranchers, and meat packers have prevented any major change in the law. (Lobbies are special interest groups that try to promote favorable legislation (or defeat unfavorable legislation) by influencing legislators and other public officials.)

THE ANIMAL WELFARE ACT

The next major federal law to affect animals was the Animal Welfare Act. Congress passed it after animal welfare groups such as the ASPCA and the Humane Society of the United States exposed the conditions under which many laboratory animals live.

The act, which has been amended several times since its initial passage in 1966, sets standards for the treatment of animals used in research, zoos, circuses, and pet stores. It covers such issues as housing, food, cleanliness, and medical care. The act also states that animals used in medical research must be given drugs to prevent pain and suffering, unless the experiment depends on measurement of the animal's pain. For example, if a researcher is studying the effects of a painkiller, it may be acceptable under the Animal Welfare Act to inflict pain on an animal, then administer the painkiller to see how well it works.[5]

The Animal Welfare Act requires that researchers keep accurate records on how animals are used in research. They must report how many animals were used in experiments, how many were given drugs, and how many experienced no pain or distress at all.

In addition to following these laws, most research institutes must also follow the *Guide for the Care and Use of Laboratory Animals*, which contains standards set by the National Institutes of Health (NIH). Any institution receiving Public Health Service funding must follow these standards. This regulation covers 90 percent of all basic research and 66 percent of all clinical research, which is directly linked to patients' health. Under these regulations, committees monitor the use of animals in research.[6]

Animal rights activists, however, are not satisfied with current regulations. They point out that mice and rats, which account for 70 percent of the animals used in experiments, are not covered by current regulations. In addition, they say, the regulations are not strictly enforced. The Society for Animal Protective Legislation alleges that in 1988, 25 percent of all licensed animal dealers were never inspected by the United States Department of Agriculture (USDA), the agency responsible for enforcing the regulations. To correct this situation, legislation was introduced in Congress in 1990 to provide another $12 million for enforcement. However, 1990 was a budget-tightening year. Since Congress did not think the country could afford the extra $12 million, the bill was defeated.[7]

In an attempt to strengthen and expand current regulations, another activist group, the Animal Legal Defense Fund (ALDF) sued the USDA. The lawsuit charged that the USDA had not set strict standards for exercising laboratory dogs or for regulating the social conditions of primates used in experiments (such as limiting their time in isolation). Congress had directed the USDA to add these additional standards when it passed amendments to the Animal Welfare Act in 1985. In August 1990, the USDA published the proposed standards for dogs and primates. In response, the USDA received more than 10,000 comments, many from researchers saying the new regulations were too expensive and interfered with science. The USDA is rewriting the standards.[8]

ABOVE THE LAW
Frustrated by the slow pace of change, some animal rights groups have performed illegal acts in an effort to "liberate" (set loose) animals in laboratories and on fur farms. The Animal Liberation Front (ALF) is the most notable of these groups. Founded in England in 1976, ALF now has an active membership in the United States. As of January 1993, the organization takes credit for 86 raids on biomedical facilities, research labs, and fur farms since its founding in the United States in 1982.[9] ALF has firebombed or vandal-

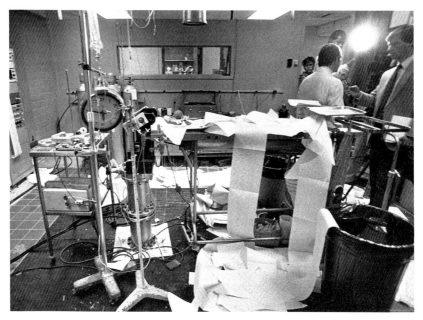

The Animal Liberation Front claims responsibility for the theft of records and the damage done at the University of Pennsylvania's animal research lab.

ized other targets. At Texas Tech University, for example, ALF members destroyed a researcher's laboratory, stole five cats, and sent the researcher a condom that they reported had been contaminated with the AIDS virus. The researchers had been using cats to study Sudden Infant Death Syndrome (SIDS), the leading killer of children under the age of one.[10]

Actions such as this one have earned ALF a place on the Federal Bureau of Investigation's (FBI's) list of domestic terrorists. Researchers, as well as most other law-abiding citizens, believe that ALF members are nothing but unethical vandals. How can people who claim to care about the rights of animals be so destructive and abuse the rights of others? Even many animal welfare groups say that such actions actually hurt their cause. ALF members, however, believe such acts are the only way to get meaningful change in this society.

WHAT LIES AHEAD?

One can only guess if and how animal protection laws will change. The United States faces a huge budget deficit and has many citizens who suffer from hunger and homelessness and who cannot afford medical care. Many people are reluctant to support costly laws to protect animals while such bad conditions exist for humans.

At the University of California's Riverside campus, a group of animal rights activists removed 260 laboratory animals and painted graffiti on the walls.

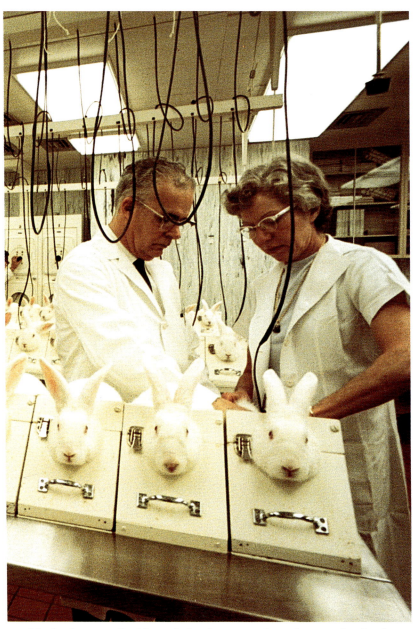

Much of our medical knowledge has come from the use of animals.

ANIMALS AND MEDICAL RESEARCH

In 1984 the world awoke to astonishing news. Doctors at La Loma Medical Center in California had transplanted the heart of a baboon into a two-year-old child, called "Baby Fae" to protect her identity. The child died a few days later. The operation was controversial in many ways. Some people hailed it as a medical miracle. Others called it unholy to mingle the body parts of human and nonhuman animals. Still others protested the fact that the baboon had been used for what they considered a hopeless operation. This medical development raised an important question: What is the role of animals in medicine and medical research?

THE CASE FOR USING ANIMALS IN MEDICAL RESEARCH

In 1796 an English doctor named Edward Jenner introduced the first effective vaccine against smallpox. Smallpox is a disease that causes victims to suffer high fever and sores all over their bodies. Hundreds of millions of people died from the disease, and millions of others were blinded or badly scarred.

Dr. Jenner noticed that dairy workers who became infected with cowpox, a less severe version of the disease, became immune to smallpox. Cowpox caused a few sores on the victim's hands but carried little danger of disfigurement or death. In a risky experiment, Jenner took some matter from sores on the hand of Sarah Nelmes, a dairy worker who had become infected with cowpox while milking cows. Jenner then made two cuts on the arm of James Phipps, a healthy eight-year-old boy, and inserted the matter from one of Nelmes's cowpox sores. The boy caught cowpox. Several weeks later, Jenner inserted smallpox matter into James Phipps in the same way.

Phipps never got smallpox, and the cowpox injection turned out to be the first vaccination. Since the discovery of the smallpox vaccine, researchers have used animals to develop vaccines for such diseases as polio, tetanus, whooping cough, and measles. Without these vaccines, a huge number of people would have died from these diseases.[1]

Much of our medical knowledge has come from the use of animals. The early vivisections—the cutting open of living animals—of the 17th century provided an understanding of some basic principles of biology. Vivisection and dissection of animals continues to shed light on biological functions, such as how the stomach absorbs food or how the brain sends messages to other parts of the body. Much of the information in biology textbooks is due, in large part, to the use of animals in biological research.

Biomedical scientists use animals to help them learn about the nature of diseases and abnormalities and to help find cures for them. Such research saves thousands, perhaps millions, of lives. In the 1950s, the first kidney

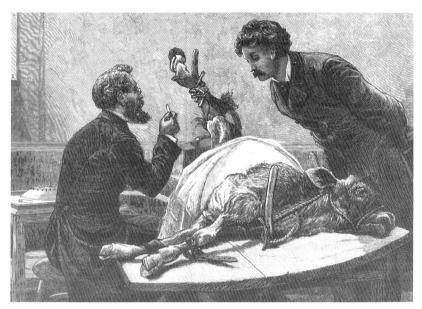

Scientists draw serum from a calf to use as an antitoxin.

transplants were done on dogs. Because of this research, kidney transplants have become relatively safe for humans. These transplants now have a success rate of 95 percent. More than 6,000 people in the United States alone are currently on a waiting list for a new kidney.[2]

The increased survival rate among cancer patients can also be attributed to animal research. In the 1930s, less than one in five people with cancer was still alive five years after diagnosis. Now almost half of all cancer patients live at least five years. This survival rate is due in part to more than 30 anticancer drugs that were tested thoroughly on animals before being used on humans. Radiation therapy for cancer has been refined through tests on rats and mice. And many surgical procedures, such as the removal of tumors, were first tested on dogs and monkeys.[3]

Treatment for kidney disease and cancer are just two examples of the benefits of animal research. Researchers credit animals with playing an important role in research on nutrition, open-heart surgery, modern anesthesia, prevention and treatment of high blood pressure, ulcers, leprosy, and many other areas of medical science.

Animals are also used by pharmaceutical companies to produce drugs and health supplements. For example, many multivitamin tablets contain vitamin E, which is extracted from beef liver. Horses are used to produce a serum for cholera, an intestinal disease that causes severe vomiting, diarrhea, and even death.[4]

A great deal of medical research also benefits animals. More than 80 medicines developed for humans are also used to treat pets and farm animals.[5] Pacemakers, devices that keep the heart beating, are being used in dogs and

Researchers at the National Cancer Institute enclose human cancer cells in microscopic capsules and grow them in laboratory mice, which are then treated with test drugs.

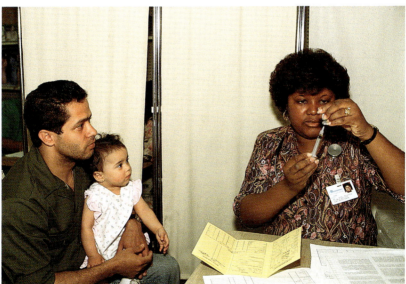

Animals as well as people benefit from medical research. The cat, top, has diabetes and must be treated with insulin. Because of early childhood innoculations, many diseases can be prevented, bottom.

cats as well as in humans. Many animals now receive chemotherapy to treat cancer, just as humans do.

Most people in the medical community believe strongly in the value of animal research and want it to continue. In 1988 the American Medical Association (AMA) surveyed doctors and scientists and found that 97 percent supported the use of animals in basic and clinical research, and 96 percent supported the use of animals for drug testing.[6]

Without the use of animals in research, humankind's hope for preventing and curing many illnesses could be dampened. Many research projects would end. For example, mice are now being used in research to determine the genetic causes of heart attacks. Studies on rats are helping researchers find a way to develop and use artificial blood. Sharks are being used to find the link between excess vitamins and cataracts, an eye disease that causes impaired vision and blindness.

Members of Incurably Ill for Animal Research (iiFAR) also support the current use of animals in medical research. Members of iiFAR include people who stand to benefit the most from animal experimentation—those with diseases that have so far been incurable. They believe that banning the use of animals in research would only further delay the discovery of cures for AIDS, cystic fibrosis, multiple sclerosis, Alzheimer's disease, and other serious health problems. For these people, animal research is an avenue of hope that could someday lead to a healthy, normal life.

DOES MEDICAL RESEARCH REQUIRE CRUELTY TO ANIMALS?

In 1985 members of ALF made public several videotapes that had been stolen from a research lab at the University of Pennsylvania. The 60 hours of videotape showed baboons, with their heads cemented into plastic helmets, being knocked unconscious by a blow to the head. The tapes also showed baboons coming out of anesthesia while surgeons were still operating on their brains.

The investigation that followed revealed that the researchers had been given money from the federal government to conduct these experiments. They were supposed to have given the baboons painkillers before any injuries were inflicted. Although funding was stopped for this particular experiment, the question of cruelty to animals in research became a serious concern.[7]

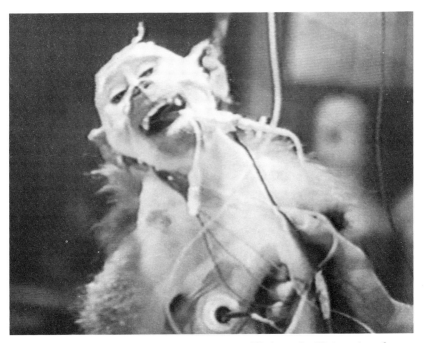

ALF members entered the Head Injury Clinic at the University of Pennsylvania and removed 60 hours of videotape that showed experiments in progress. The group claims that the baboons, like the one above, were not adequately anesthetized during the experiments.

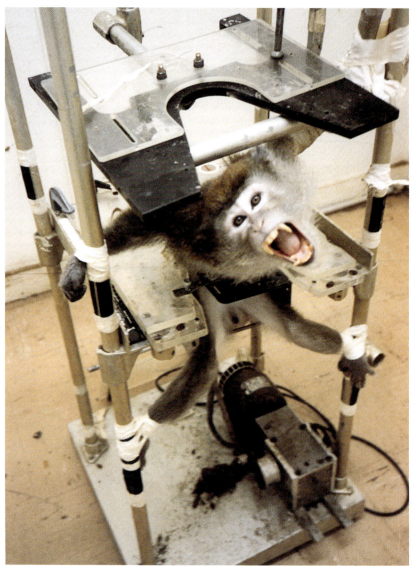

When police raided a laboratory run by the Institute for Behavioral Research in Silver Spring, Maryland, researcher Edward Taub, Ph.D., was charged with animal cruelty. Strapped into restraining devices like the one above, the monkeys used in various experiments suffered extreme pain and stress.

A cranial electrode is implanted in the head of this cat. ALF members claim the cat's left eye shows signs of nerve damage to brain cells.

Animal rights literature is filled with stories of alleged animal abuse in medical research. One article reports that monkeys at the Armed Forces Radiobiology Institute in Bethesda, Maryland, were used in an experiment to test the effects of radiation. The monkeys were exposed to various doses of radiation and then forced to run on a treadmill. Monkeys that stopped running on the treadmills were given electric shocks to keep them moving. Some monkeys that vomited violently during this experiment were given increasingly painful shocks to keep them moving. Some of the monkeys did not die for more than five days.[8]

Another PETA publication shows dozens of photographs of animals used in research. One kitten is shown with an electrode implanted in its head and a gaping wound surrounding the implant. Other photos show dogs, one with its skin burned off in an experiment, and another dog, used in research on the relationship between smoking and lung cancer, is being forced to breathe nicotine-laden smoke through a tube in its throat.[9]

Animal rights activists want to see a commonly used research test, the Lethal Dose 50 (LD 50), outlawed. The test is used primarily to test potentially dangerous chemicals and new drugs. Designed in the 1920s, the classical LD 50 test

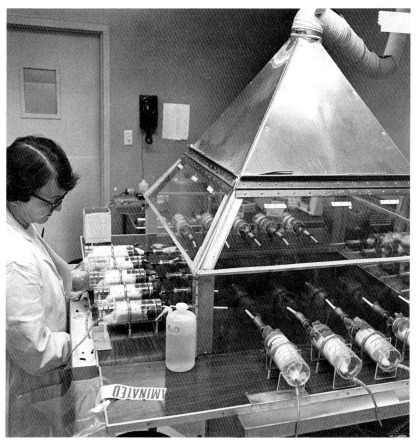

Rats are forced to smoke cigarettes during a laboratory test.

calls for researchers to administer the substance in question to 100 lab animals. The dosage is increased until 50 of the animals die—hence the name "Lethal Dose 50."

Many researchers say that most claims of cruelty are sensational, misleading, or both. In response to objections to the LD 50, Sandra Bressler, Director of the California Biomedical Association, says that very few researchers use the classical LD 50 test anymore. If a test for the lethality of a substance is necessary, researchers use as few as six subjects per test. The animals are euthanized (killed in a painless way) as soon as they show signs of serious illness. She points out that the Food and Drug Administration requires that a food, drug, or chemical be proved safe before it can be used on humans. At this time, the LD 50 test is the only valid test—meaning that it is reliable, accurate, and available. Without testing on animals first, there is a great risk that human lives would be in danger.[10]

Researchers who favor animal testing insist that most animals are comfortable during research procedures. In 1988 the United States Department of Agriculture reported that 95 percent of all animals in federally funded facilities do not experience pain or distress. Of the remaining animals, most were involved in pain studies. Pain relievers or anesthesia were administered to these animals as soon as it was appropriate to do so.[11]

Most animal researchers also follow guidelines set by the federal government to give animals good care while in captivity. Every institution that receives federal funding or is licensed with the U.S. Department of Agriculture has an active Animal Care and Use Committee. This committee includes at least one veterinarian and one person who is not a part of the institution. The committee verifies that ani-

Animal rights activists seek alternatives to the use of animals in medical research.

mal research is necessary and appropriate when used. It also makes sure the species being tested is appropriate and sees that no animals experience unnecessary pain or discomfort.[12]

Animal rights activists dispute the validity of such claims and statistics. They estimate that between 17 and 22 million animals are used each year in medical research. They also point out that the USDA statistics do not include experiments on rats, mice, fish, and farm animals. That could mean that up to 90 percent of all research animals are not included in the statistics.[13] Animal rights activists also claim that there are not enough inspectors to verify that labs are following regulations.

What is the solution? Some animal welfare advocates would like to see animals used sparingly and only in painless experiments when absolutely necessary. However, many animal rights activists believe that animals are no longer needed in medical research. They believe that researchers have many alternatives available to them and that these alternatives should be used.

WHAT ARE THE ALTERNATIVES?

A few alternatives to animal testing do exist. According to most researchers, however, such alternatives have limitations. For example, microorganisms can sometimes be exposed to chemicals to determine whether a substance is poisonous or carcinogenic (cancer-causing). The Ames test uses salmonellae, single-celled organisms that have no nervous system and can therefore feel no pain. In the 1980s, this test helped prove that chemicals used to treat fabric in children's sleepwear were unsafe.[14]

As another alternative, researchers sometimes use cell and tissue cultures extracted from humans or animals rather than expose a whole animal to testing. If they are not already naturally diseased, the cells in a piece of extracted tissue can then be exposed to disease or untested drugs. The National Cancer Institute is now using one such test to screen new anticancer drugs. Before this alternative was developed, mice were given leukemia and treated with various drugs. Now the same drugs are tested on live human cancer cells in a test tube. This program has reduced the number of animals used in anticancer drug testing from 6,000,000 to less than 300,000 per year.[15]

Another alternative involves the use of mathematical or computer models to simulate cell reactions and biological functions. For example, a researcher may be trying to find a drug that will work against a disease-causing enzyme. By using formulas and graphics, a computer can show researchers where and how the enzyme attacks the human body. The researcher can then see how certain drugs might block the enzyme.[16]

In recent years, a number of bills have been introduced in Congress to prohibit tests such as the LD 50 and to force researchers to use alternative testing procedures when possible. To date, these bills have been defeated at both the state and the national levels. State Senator Margaret Schweinhaut of Maryland supported such a bill at first, then voted against it. After talking with researchers, she came to believe that tests such as the LD 50 are in the best interest of public safety, since most alternatives are not 100 percent reliable. She said that she did not want to "be in the position where I supported the idea that animals come first and humans come second."[17]

Many researchers say that alternatives to animal testing are indeed promising and attractive. Using microorganisms and cell cultures is often less costly for researchers than keeping animals in the laboratory. But the reliability of all these alternatives is still debatable. Researchers caution that tests done with cell and tissue cultures can be misleading. Such tests cannot be used to predict how all the parts of a human or animal biological system will react to a drug. Although alternative methods of testing may reduce the number of animals used in research, animals are still the most reliable subjects with which to test the safety and effectiveness of a drug.[18]

THE FEDERAL FOOD, DRUG, AND COSMETIC ACT
In 1937 a drug called Elixir Sulfanilamide went on the U.S. market. Two months later, more than 100 people in 15 states

Ryan White, a seventh-grade student, died of AIDS. Without using animals, will researchers find a cure for this and other diseases?

had died from taking the drug, which contained a chemical traditionally used as an antifreeze. As a result, Congress passed the Federal Food, Drug, and Cosmetic Act of 1938, which requires that any new drug be proved safe before it can be sold in the United States.[19]

No one wants to see human tragedy result from using unsafe food, chemicals, or drugs, and no one wants to limit the medical options available to both human and non-human animals. Most people in the medical community and the patients they treat are in favor of using animals in relevant medical research. Animal welfare advocates want to see that animals are used in humane, painless experiments, only when absolutely necessary for public safety. Many animal rights activists want to see all animal testing stopped and more money and energy used to develop valid, nonanimal tests. Any amount of cruelty to animals is too much, say the activists. Real cruelty, say the researchers, is letting humans die needlessly.

ANIMALS AND AGRICULTURE

In the late 1980s, the National Livestock and Meat Board hired actors, including James Garner, to appear in commercials promoting beef as "real food for real people." The Meat Board, which represents livestock owners, marketers, and retailers, intended to promote beef as a healthy, wholesome food. The ad campaign was done because the popularity of beef has declined in recent years, primarily because medical researchers found that eating too much red meat was linked to high cholesterol and heart disease. The consumption of beef has dropped by almost one-third since 1976.[1]

Members of PETA want to see the popularity of beef decline even further—but not only because of health concerns. In 1990 PETA hired country singer k.d. lang to do commercials as part of their "Meat Stinks" campaign. The singer's words, "If you knew how meat was made, you'd probably lose your lunch," focused the public's attention on alleged cruelty in the meat industry. In response many radio stations in Oklahoma, Kansas, Missouri, and Nebraska—cattle-producing states—boycotted lang's music. They opposed her view of the cattle and meat industries, which provide employment for many people in those states.[2]

PETA's objection to meat, and that of some other activist and animal welfare groups, is due in part to their objection to large, automated farms. Animal rights activists often call such farms "factory farms," and they believe that animals involved in such operations receive cruel treatment. People in agribusiness—those who run large, automated farms—call it "intensive farming."

At Maybury State Park in Northville, Michigan, state officials have set up what they call a "living farm." A walk through the farm provides visitors with a look at life on an old-fashioned family farm. Geese and ducks swim in a large pond, cows graze in spacious pastures, and pigs lie in their pens. Dozens of hens roost together in a small shed, laying their eggs where they please. A farm employee throws the animals hay and grain that are grown on the farm and frequently pets the animals or calls them by name.

Farms like the one in Maybury State Park were once quite common. With such an operation, a farmer could generally raise enough food to feed four or five people. Some small farms still exist, but they are not responsible for the great amount of food produced in the United States. Large family-owned and company-owned farms are responsible for that accomplishment. As farming became less common as a way of life, it became more and more important as a business. Less than three percent of all Americans now live on farms, yet production is greater than ever before.[3]

With new fertilizers and improved strains of seeds, farmers in the United States can grow more than seven billion bushels of corn and two billion bushels of wheat each year.[4] The development of genetics, the science that explains how

Sometimes chicken houses have several tiers to maximize the use of space.

physical characteristics are inherited, allowed farmers to improve breeding methods. Improved livestock feeds, mechanization of feeding and slaughtering techniques, and advances in veterinary medicine further increased productivity. American farmers can now produce 99 million head of cattle, 54 million pigs, and more than 5 billion chickens each year.[5]

THE BENEFITS OF INTENSIVE FARMING

To get such high productivity for the lowest cost, farmers use automation whenever possible. In a typical broiler chicken farm, for example, baby chicks are penned in

Many people believe it is wrong to eat meat. Others would find it difficult to give it up. The average American consumes 100 pounds of red meat each year.

groups of 10,000 or more. Sometimes the chicken houses have tiers to maximize the use of space. Food and water are dropped automatically from feeders located in the roof of the pen. Adding small amounts of antibiotics and growth hormones to the food prevents disease that might otherwise occur and increases the rate of growth. The chickens are usually ready for the market in about seven weeks.[6]

The average American, who eats more than 100 pounds of red meat and 60 pounds of poultry each year, benefits financially from large, efficiently run, automated farms. Not only do American farmers provide more than enough food for the United States, they also export more than $5 billion worth of meat, eggs, skins, and animal fats to other countries.[7] Many people believe that without modern farming techniques, farms would not be profitable, American eating habits would change drastically, and people in other countries would be denied products they desire. Large, automated farms are efficient and do what they are supposed to do—provide food to a large number of people.

DOES INTENSIVE FARMING MEAN CRUELTY TO ANIMALS?

In chapter 2, you read that many animal rights activists believe that animals and humans deserve equal consideration, or even equal treatment. For the strictest animal rights activists, raising any animal to be killed and eaten is cruel. They believe that both humans and animals have a right to life. In their view, vegetarianism is the only way to ensure this right.

Many animal welfare groups have no objection to animals being raised for food, but they object to the methods used to raise and slaughter them. For example, the Humane

Farming Association (HFA), a nonprofit organization of public health specialists, veterinarians, consumer advocates, and family farmers, says its members "are united in a campaign to protect consumers from the dangerous misuse of chemicals in food production and to eliminate the severe and senseless suffering to which farm animals are subjected."[8] One of the HFA's most recent and visible campaigns has been against the methods used by many large farms to raise milk-fed calves for veal.

About one million milk-fed calves are raised in the United States each year. These calves are taken away from their mothers when they are a few days old and placed in crates that are approximately 22 inches wide and 58 inches long. The calves are fed low-iron milk for 14–16 weeks, then they are sent to market for slaughter. Because of their diet and

These milk-fed calves are raised for their tender, flavorful meat, called veal.

lack of exercise, the calves grow to 300 pounds or more by slaughter time. The meat from these calves, called veal, is pale white in color, very tender, and flavorful.

Animal rights activists and the HFA say that the trade-off for the human consumption of white veal is the comfort and health of the animals. The crates they are kept in, says the HFA, are too small for the animals to turn around in. Eventually, the cramped quarters and the lack of exercise cripple many calves. The low-iron milk diet results in diarrhea and anemia. The HFA and many animal rights groups are calling for consumers to boycott veal.[9]

In his book *Inhumane Society,* Dr. Michael Fox claims that the crowded conditions on "factory farms" lead to high stress in animals that causes violent behavior. To reduce fighting, farmers often use a laser instrument to cut off the top beaks of hens. According to Fox, piglets often have their tails amputated (called tail docking) to prevent tail biting and cannibalism.[10]

THE RESPONSE OF THE ANIMAL INDUSTRY

According to the Animal Industry Foundation (AIF), "one of the best strongholds of animal welfare in our culture is the farmer."[11] The foundation claims that the treatment animals receive on large, automated farms is actually more humane than treatment received on a small, family-run operation. On small farms, animals are raised primarily outdoors, where they are exposed to bad weather and extreme temperatures, predators, and disease. On most large farms, animals are sheltered and receive the best food and health care possible. The foundation points out that if animals were truly stressed, they would not become fat, lay eggs, or give milk.[12]

Intensive farming methods increase productivity, but many people wonder whether the animals suffer from cramped living conditions.

In response to accusations about the treatment of veal calves, the foundation says that modern farmers house their animals in clean, well-lighted barns, where the calves have room to lie down in their stalls and can see other calves. Their diet consists of milk fortified with minerals, vitamins, and "animal health products." Contradicting the HFA, the Animal Industry Foundation insists that the low-iron content of the milk does not hurt the calves' health.[13]

Likewise, other practices that animal rights groups view as cruel are thought by the AIF to be kind and done only to protect the animals. For example, the practice of debeaking chickens protects them from their own natural tendencies to attack each other. Chickens establish their rank in the flock, often called the "pecking order," by fighting. Once established, the strongest bird gets to eat first, the next strongest goes next, and so on. Debeaking the chickens eliminates the possibility of injury as they engage in natural behaviors.

The AIF also says that farmers amputate, or dock, pigs' tails for the animals' protection. Animal rights groups claim that pigs on large farms try to bite off each other's tails because confinement frustrates them. But a recent study at Texas Tech University found that tail biting occurred among animals raised in dirt lots as well, though somewhat less frequently than with confined pigs. This evidence indicates that confinement is not the only cause of tail biting.[14]

IS THE FOOD HEALTHY?

Animal rights advocates argue that the meat from large, automated farms is unhealthy. Food hormones and antibiotics are given regularly to confined animals to foster growth and ward off disease. In 1988, $2.5 million was spent on drugs for animals in the United States.[15]

As a consequence, high residues of these drugs are sometimes found in meat. The USDA reports that milk-fed veal is three times more likely to contain illegal levels of antibiotic residue than all other varieties of veal. In some cases, residue levels have been 500 times over the legal limit. Sulfamethazine, a known cancer-causing chemical, has also been found in milk-fed veal.[16] Many animal rights groups fear that a human's health may be endangered by eating such veal.

Animal rights groups also argue that the USDA cannot adequately check all meats for drug residue. In 1989, for example, tests were done on only 1 of every 2,000 cattle, 1 of every 6,660 hogs, 1 of every 50,000 turkeys, and 1 of a million chickens.[17] Because most farms are so large, regulation sometimes seems impossible. Many animal rights activists believe the only answer is to scale down or eliminate what they refer to as the factory farm.

People who successfully operate large farms don't deny that they use drugs on animals, but they claim that the drugs are necessary to safeguard the animals from disease. The drugs, they say, would be required whether the animals were raised in shelters or outside. They also scoff at the idea that these drugs are dangerous to humans. The FDA regulates the type and amount of antibiotics that can be given to animals. Some of the antibiotics given to animals are the same as those prescribed for humans. The FDA denies claims that its inspections are inadequate.[18]

Farmers who operate large, automated farms also insist that no proof exists that the drugs or growth hormones used in animals cause cancer or other illnesses in humans. In fact, they say that meat is healthy for humans. Red meat is the only complete source of all 10 essential amino acids, a group of organic compounds that are necessary for the proper functioning of the human body. Although recent studies indicate that eating too much red meat can be a health risk, eliminating red meat altogether can also be a health risk if a meatless diet is not properly balanced. Until meat is proved unhealthy, it will probably remain a part of the average American's basic diet.[19]

ARE LARGE FARMS
ENVIRONMENTALLY SOUND?

Some environmentalists also object to large-scale farming. The Worldwatch Institute, a Washington, D.C.-based environmental research organization, says that it takes 5 pounds of grain, 2,500 gallons of water, the energy equivalent of a gallon of gasoline, and 35 pounds of eroded topsoil to pro-

Meat and eggs are inspected by workers from the U.S. Department of Agriculture.

Many urban dwellers almost never see cattle except as packaged meat. Ranchers probably have a different view.

duce a 1-pound steak.[20] Other statistics indicate that livestock consumes half the crops grown and over half the water consumed in the United States each year. They compare that to the 480 gallons of water needed to produce soybeans, which are often used as a meat substitute.[21]

Many environmentalists argue that the land, water, and grain used to feed cattle would be better used to raise soybeans, rice, wheat, corn, and other grains. The crops would feed more people in what they consider a more environmentally sound way.

Animal farmers take the opposite view. They believe that if they stopped raising cattle, the result could be an ecological disaster. Jeremy Rifkin, an environmentalist whose book *Beyond Beef: The Rise and Fall of the Cattle Culture,* cites India as a model country that does not raise cattle for food. In much of India, cattle are not eaten because of religious reasons. Rifkin does not mention that many of India's

200 million cows are starving and are constantly searching for food.[22]

Farmers also point out that the high beef production in the United States is a direct result of consumer demand. Red meat and poultry are the third most frequently consumed foods in this country. They see the reduction or elimination of meat intake as an intrusion on the personal choices and rights of American consumers.

WHAT LIES AHEAD?

What is the future of large, automated farms? Of the 2.2 million farms in the United States, 87 percent are owned by an individual or a married couple responsible for operating the farm. Only 7,000 farms are owned by corporations.[23] Nevertheless, animal rights activists criticize the animal industry and the American public's taste for meat. Jeremy Rifkin is mobilizing environmental and animal rights groups to call for a 50 percent reduction in beef consumption over the next 20 years.[24] The Humane Farming Association helped bring the California Veal Protection Act to Congress in 1990, a bill that would require more space for calves and a diet with adequate iron. The bill was defeated by a narrow margin.[25]

Many environmental and animal rights groups hope that, in time, the United States will follow the lead of the European Economic Community, which has recently banned the routine feeding of antibiotics to livestock.[26]

These children are protesting the use of animals to test consumer products before they are put on the market.

ANIMALS IN THE FASHION & COSMETICS INDUSTRIES

Animals have long played a part in the human quest to look beautiful and fashionable. For example, the early Egyptians concocted beauty creams for the skin. The creams were made of 90 percent animal fat and 10 percent balsam, a plant resin. Ancient Babylonians ground dried insects called cochineal into a red paste used to color the lips.[1]

In western Europe during the Middle Ages (about 500–1500 A.D.), animal skins became a symbol of wealth and fashion. At that time, royalty and the upper class began to wear ermine, otter, sable, and fox to emphasize their social position.[2] To name just a few examples, the plumes of peacocks and ostriches, the skins of cows and eels, and the ivory tusks of elephants have been used in the name of fashion.

THE USE OF ANIMALS IN COSMETICS

Of all the animals used in laboratory testing, about one percent are used for cosmetics and consumer home product testing.[3] Everyday products, such as eye shadow, hairspray, face cream, and shampoo, are tested to ensure that they will not cause irritation or severe damage to the skin, eyes, or internal system when used by humans.

The two primary tests used for cosmetics are the LD 50 (see chapter 4) and the Draize test. The Draize test was developed in the 1940s by Dr. J. H. Draize of the Food and Drug Administration to test eye irritants. The need for such a test became evident when an untested product called Lash Lure came on the U.S. market in 1933. Lash Lure was an eyelash dye. Women who accidentally got the substance in their eyes suffered permanent eye damage.[4]

The Draize test usually requires six rabbits. The researcher puts a yoke around the neck of each rabbit, immobilizes its legs, and places a solid or liquid substance, such as shampoo, on the rabbit's lower eyelid. Rabbits are used for these tests because they can't blink and wash away the substances and also because they are generally passive and easy to work with. The researcher observes the rabbits' eyes for several days. In some cases, the substances are harmless, but sometimes the rabbits' eyes may swell or bleed, or the rabbits may become blind.[5]

Animal rights activists want to eliminate the Draize test because they believe it is cruel and that alternative tests exist. For example, Avon, one of the first companies to develop a "cruelty free" policy, uses cell cultures and Eyetex, a test developed as an alternative to animal testing. Eyetex is a synthetic protein substance that reacts to chemicals almost like eyes do.[6]

Many other companies also boast products that have been developed without animal testing. Animal rights activists point out that if some companies can do this, all should follow suit. Animal rights and many animal welfare groups advocate consumer boycotts against cosmetic companies that use animals to test their products, and this technique has had some success. For example, after the Animal Rights Coalition put an ad in the *New York Times* asking, "How many rabbits does Revlon blind for beauty's sake?" the company committed itself to "cruelty free" cosmetics. In this way, animal rights activists hope to eliminate the use of the Draize test.

THE DEBATE ABOUT ALTERNATIVES

Proponents of the Draize test do not oppose alternatives to animal testing, but they say that using alternatives is not a simple matter. The Food and Drug Administration requires cosmetics companies to use approved ingredients, to follow specific labeling guidelines on packages, and to test products for safety. The FDA does not specify what test should be used, which means that cosmetics companies are self-regulated in matters related to testing. They are responsible for doing whatever is necessary to ensure the safety of a product. If an unsafe product goes on the market, the FDA will recall the product, and legal action may be taken against the company.

Until the last few years, the Draize test has been the only test that cosmetics companies felt was valid and reliable. According to Kevin Renskers, director of toxicology for Avon, finding valid alternatives to the Draize test requires a great commitment of time and money. At Avon, Eyetex was tested many times on more than 500 different products before it was considered valid and reliable. However, a test that has been validated for one company's products will not necessarily be valid for similar products made by another

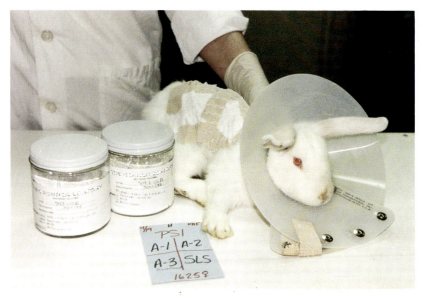

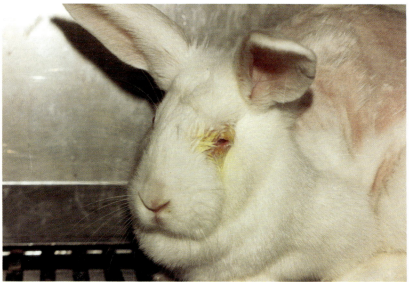

Many cosmetics companies test their products on rabbits to prevent possible skin damage to humans. These companies often rely on the Draize test, although it can irritate a rabbit's eyes and sometimes cause blindness.

company. Renskers says that each company that wants to use Eyetex must perform the validation tests on each of its own products. Even then there is no guarantee that the results will be satisfactory.[7]

Those who use the Draize test say they are doing so out of concern for human safety. Until they are 100 percent sure of alternatives, they will continue to use the Draize. They believe that it is better to risk the eyes of a rabbit than the eyes of a person.

THE FIGHT AGAINST FUR

The debate about using animals extends beyond cosmetics to the fashion industry. In 1990 Mayor Bill Stirling proposed that the town of Aspen, Colorado, prohibit the sale of animal furs within its boundaries. Aspen has several ski resorts, and many celebrities and other wealthy people who wear fur go there to ski every year.

The residents of Aspen were divided on the question. Some animal rights groups argued that there was no practical need for fur anymore. Most ski clothing is made from synthetic materials that are warm, waterproof, and lightweight. Animal rights activists believe that fur serves only as a fashion statement, and the demand for it causes cruelty to animals. To dramatize their point, they put up posters with pictures of fur-bearing animals with their legs caught in steel traps. The words on the poster said, "Fur. It's Not a Pretty Business."

Another group, which included some of the owners of Aspen's clothing stores and ski resorts, thought that a prohibition on fur would hurt their businesses. They feared that wealthy customers would no longer come to Aspen if they could not buy furs or wear the furs they already

Many people feel that animal rights activists interfere with an individual's personal choice to wear fur.

owned. Others balked at the idea of a personal choice being taken away by the government. A pro-fur advertisement read: "Today fur. Tomorrow leather. Then wool. Then meat."[8] Eventually the measure was voted down by a two to one margin.[9]

For animal rights groups, the issue is still alive and worthy of debate. They do not think animals should be used for human purposes. They also want to eliminate practices that they believe cause the needless suffering of animals—practices that include trapping, hunting, and raising animals for their fur. Animal rights activists view such practices as senseless and cruel. Those who make their living from the fur industry and those who choose to wear fur think otherwise. They maintain that raising and killing animals for their fur is an honest and natural way to make a living. They believe that the choice to wear fur is a personal one that should be decided by individuals and not by laws.

In the United States, approximately 70 million animals are killed each year for their fur. About 30 million of them,* including raccoons, muskrats, and beavers, are trapped in the wild by a steel-jaw leghold trap, a device that clamps down on the animal's legs and immobilizes it until the trapper retrieves it. Then the animal is killed, usually by drowning or clubbing.[10]

Animal rights and animal welfare groups vigorously oppose the use of such traps. They claim that 25 percent of the animals caught with these traps chew off their own legs in an effort to escape. Then they often bleed to death. Sometimes the animals wait days before the trapper comes to retrieve them.[11]

Furs also come from fur farms, where animals are raised for their pelts and other by-products. Mink oil, for example,

Steel-jaw leghold traps immobilize an animal until it can be retrieved by a trapper.

is a key ingredient in many hypoallergenic cosmetics. Mink, chinchillas, and foxes make up the bulk of animals raised on fur farms. Like other farmers, fur farmers want to produce the greatest number of animals for the least amount of cost. They also point out that it is in their interest to treat their animals humanely. On a mink farm, between one and four animals are housed in a one-foot by three-foot enclosure.[12] When they are ready for the market, the animals are usually gassed with either carbon monoxide or carbon dioxide—the same procedure that veterinarians use for euthanizing household pets when necessary. The method is painless and keeps the animals' pelts clean and undamaged.

Although animal rights groups oppose hunting, trapping, and fur farming, many people think these groups are

Fur farms have caused a decrease in the number of fur-bearing animals that are trapped. In many areas of the country, the overpopulation of these animals is causing problems for people and pets.

Should people no longer have the choice to wear fur?

Nature itself can seem cruel. Is it wrong for this cheetah to feed on the deer? If not, why shouldn't humans also use animals for food?

out of touch with nature. In an article for *Outdoor Life*, Richard Conniff writes, "If we were to follow [nature's] example, we would kill whatever we wanted, whenever we wanted, by whatever means became handy."[13] Canadian trapper Bob Groves echoes this view. "Nature is a very cruel harvester," he said in a *Business Week* article. He said that when a wolf catches a beaver, "first he cuts its tendons so it can't run away. Then he slits it open and guts it alive."[14]

Conniff points out in his article that trappers are not "willfully cruel." It is in their economic interest to keep pelts in good condition. To keep animals from suffering for a prolonged period of time or mutilating themselves, many trappers work 16-hour days to retrieve animals in a timely manner. Whenever possible, trappers use underwater traps that cause the animal to drown in about one minute. Other traps snap shut around the animal's neck and cause instant death. These traps are becoming more and more common.

For a long time, trapping has been viewed as an acceptable way to control wildlife. The Department of the Interior uses more than 20,000 steel traps on public lands in order to control mountain lions, bobcats, and other predators considered dangerous. When trapping is done within regulated limits, trappers maintain that they are doing their part to control animal populations.[15] Many people resent animal rights activists who want to eliminate the jobs of trappers. And they resent the idea of someone taking away their choice to wear fur.

Animal rights activists, however, continue publicity campaigns against buying and wearing fur. They have used celebrity spokespersons, such as the Oakland A's manager Tony LaRussa and actress Candice Bergen. Animal rights groups hope to lessen consumer demand, and statistics indicate that their campaigns may have an effect. Activists point out that the number of trappers in the United States has decreased from 500,000 to 100,000 since 1986. Others, however, point out that the decrease is due to ranch mink flooding the market and causing fur prices in general to fall.[16] In the past, the consumer has generally been the one who settled which and how many animals were used for fur clothing. Animal rights activists hope that in the future, legislators will pass laws to protect animals from being killed for their fur.

The circus comes to New York City.

ANIMALS AS ENTERTAINERS

Entertainment in ancient Rome was often violent and bloody. At the Roman Colosseum, one could see lions, tigers, bulls, snakes, and other animals fighting for their lives. For variety, slaves and soldiers were placed in the arena with the animals. On other occasions, men called gladiators fought each other to the death. Onlookers cheered, as people fought each other and the animals in pools of blood. For miles around, the crowd of 50,000 could be heard cheering for more.[1]

For many people, the thought of such a spectacle is gruesome and would never be tolerated in mainstream American society. By law, people couldn't intentionally be killed in the arena today. But what about animals? Is it permissible to use animals for the entertainment of humans if it causes pain to the animals?

THE CASE OF THE HIGH-DIVING MULES

Smokey, Dipsy, and Kit are mules—high-diving mules. For five months a year, they tour and perform at state fairs and rodeos. Their act consists of scrambling up a ramp to a small platform, then jumping 18 feet into a 6-foot-deep tank of water. Their owners and trainers, Tim and Patti Rivers, reward the mules with carrots and other treats.

The Riverses have been taken to court at least seven times by individuals or groups concerned about the welfare of the mules. Lisa Jennings, president of Sangre de Cristo Animal Protection Inc., an animal rights group in Albuquerque, New Mexico, spearheaded one of the recent court actions against the mule act. Although Jennings did not equate the mule act with the games of ancient Rome, she argued in *People* magazine that such entertainment is not worthy of a modern society. "It's just a sleazy carny act," she said. "Here we are, approaching the 21st century, and we're being entertained by diving mules."[2]

In ancient Rome, gladiators fought with animals and with each other.

Toni Conti, a concerned citizen, also objected to the treatment of the mules. When the act came to Albuquerque, she went on a 17-day hunger strike to protest against it. Although Conti is not affiliated with any animal rights or animal welfare groups, she felt that it was her duty to try to stop the mule act from continuing. She believed that for children, the act was a bad example of how animals ought to be treated. She also felt that the mules were suffering physical discomfort and stress.

The courts and the paying public were not swayed, however, and the show went on. The owners, who are maintaining a family business that was started in 1957, will continue to tour with the mules as long as they are allowed to do so. They claim that the animals are being treated humanely.

IS CRUELTY INVOLVED?
According to animal rights activists, the case of the diving mules is just one example of how animals are misused—or even abused—in the entertainment world. They believe that circuses, rodeos, dolphin acts, and bullfights are equally cruel, because animals are forced to perform in ways that are unnatural to them. Animal rights activists claim that in many cases, extreme cruelty is used to make the animals perform tricks. Circus bears, they say, are beaten with steel rods until they dance; rodeo animals suffer broken necks and legs during roping events; and chimpanzees endure shocks from an electric prod until they ride bikes and turn somersaults on command.[3]

People who use animals in the entertainment business insist that cruelty is the exception, not the rule. They point out that anticruelty laws exist to protect animals from harsh

A polar bear at the Central Park zoo arouses the interest of a young onlooker.

treatment. Acts such as the diving mules would not be allowed to continue if the public thought cruelty was involved. They argue that what activists view as entertainment actually results in public education about animals. As the public learns to appreciate animals, the animals' interests will be better served. Perhaps the best example of this is today's changing zoos.

EDUCATION OR ENTERTAINMENT?

To a majority of people, zoos provide entertainment and education. Many large, well-established zoos strive to be accredited by the American Association of Zoological Parks and Aquariums (AAZPA). Wildlife conservation is one of the main purposes of accredited zoos. Breeding animals in captivity may offer the only means of survival for many species that face extinction in nature. Zookeepers take care of the animals' needs. Most zoos employ zoologists (also called curators) and veterinarians as well. Accredited zoos also provide educational programs and tours and entertainment for people of all ages.

The current trend among larger zoos is to provide the animals with more spacious, natural environments. For example, at the Bronx Zoo's Jungle World, sounds of jungle insects and birds are broadcasted through speakers. At the San Diego Wild Animal Park, more than 2,000 wild animals roam free on 700 acres of land that resembles their African habitat. People who visit the exhibit must stay inside their monorail car. The people are entertained and the animals appear content in their natural habitats.[4]

Zoo supporters point out another benefit of natural habitats. Animals are more likely to mate in these environments, thus promoting survival of their species. A San Diego rhino

Zookeepers feed the seals as the crowd watches.

who had never mated in a confined zoo has fathered 55 off-
spring since being moved to an open environment. In more
organized efforts, some zoos have captive breeding programs. These programs assist the animals in mating and, in
some cases, returning the young to the wild, where their
species can live and breed naturally. Israel and Jordan, for
example, have received rare antelope from the San Diego
Park. And the Bronx Zoo has returned condors to the wild.
Without such programs, many species would probably become extinct.[5]

Debra Jordan, a PETA researcher, does not agree that all
"natural" zoos are good for animals. She points out that the
Buffalo Zoo spent $1 million on a "natural environment" for
its gorillas. To the public, it looks as though the animals are
free to explore through tropical trees and plants. But according to Jordan, an electrified wire separates the gorillas
from the plants. So while the exhibit looks natural, it is
meant only for the eyes of the paying public.

Jordan also believes that breeding animals in zoos is a
dangerous business. Surplus animals are sometimes sold
to animal entertainment shows, and sometimes they must
be destroyed.[6]

WILL THE SHOW GO ON?
The most radical animal rights groups would like animals
in entertainment banned altogether. Circuses can be just
as entertaining without animals, a theory tested and proved
by the "animal-free" French Canadian circus, Cirque du
Soleil. Animal rights activists will continue to hold public
protests and to lobby for legislation to see that rodeos,
whale shows, and other forms of animal entertainment become things of the past.

*Cirque du Soleil is trying to
reinvent the circus. The troupe
uses music, acrobatics, theater,
and dance—but no animals.*

Activists point to the case of the Kandu, one of San Diego
Sea World's two female orca whales. During a performance,
Kandu smashed into her partner. With her jaw broken,
Kandu thrashed in agony in front of a large crowd until she
bled to death. Kandu's death was accidental, but animal
rights groups say the accident would never have happened
if she had not been forced to perform at Sea World.

In general, however, the public seems to be in favor of
using animals as entertainers, as long as it is done without
cruelty. Attractions like Marine World and the San Diego
Zoo attract millions of paying visitors each year. These visitors enjoy watching the animals—sometimes performing
and sometimes in a natural habitat—and they want to continue to have that opportunity. As long as that's true, it
seems that the show will go on.

ANIMALS
AND INDUSTRY

People in the logging camps of the Pacific Northwest are accustomed to the buzz of chainsaws and the thunder of falling trees. The rumble of trucks hauling away felled trees is almost soothing—these sounds mean that people are working and that families are being fed.

But in the spring of 1990, a disturbing sound—the cries of protesters—was heard among the trees of Oregon, Washington, and northern California. Their mission: to save the spotted owl.

The spotted owl stands about 18 inches high, is dark brown with white spots, and has large eyes. In the 1800s, approximately 1,700 pairs of owls lived among the trees of the Pacific Northwest. By 1990 the number had dropped to half that. Environmentalists and animal rights groups feared that the spotted owl would become extinct if its habitat continued to shrink.[1]

Many biologists and wildlife experts blamed the lumber industry for the drop in the owl population. The spotted owl tends to make its home in forests of ancient Douglas firs and redwoods, called "old-growth" forests because of the age of the trees. Two federal agencies, the National Forest Service and the Bureau of Land Management sell lumber companies the right to clear-cut 70,000 acres of old-growth forest yearly.[2] When a forest is clear-cut, every tree in the area is removed. The trees are used to provide products such as lumber, plywood, particle board, and paper. The demand for these products results in thousands of jobs for loggers and others in related industries.

In 1990 conservationists called for the U.S. Fish and Wildlife Service, another federal agency, to place the spotted owl on the endangered species list. According to U.S. policy, measures would then have to be taken to save the owl. This would undoubtedly mean a halt to logging in some of the old-growth forests.

The lumber industry objected to the proposal and claimed that such a measure would result in the loss of 30,000 jobs. Many of these displaced workers would have to draw unemployment benefits before finding other jobs. Those who could not find another job would eventually draw welfare benefits. Related industries and their employees might also be adversely affected. Less wood pulp, for example, might drive up the price of paper. If the demand for paper dropped because of high prices, jobs in the paper industry might be lost. In addition, the U.S. treasury could lose up to $229 million per year in timber money.[3] To make up for such losses, the government might have to increase taxes, an unpopular move in the eyes of many Americans.

In late June, the U.S. Fish and Wildlife Service placed the spotted owl on the endangered species list. But the Bureau of Land Management agreed to reduce logging by only 15 to 20 percent, too small a reduction according to environ-

An environmental group called Earth First protests the actions of the U.S. Forest Service.

mentalists.[4] Many conservationists felt the government had sold out to the lumber industry. They believed that if logging were not limited by a greater percentage, the spotted owl and many other species of wildlife would face extinction.

The spotted owl controversy is just one example of much bigger questions in the debate about animal rights. Should a product or an industry be limited when the survival of a species is at stake? And should wildlife be preserved even when preservation causes economic hardship, such as the loss of jobs, to humans?

IS CONSERVATION OF WILDLIFE NECESSARY?

Not all scientists believe in conservation. Some believe extinction is a normal part of evolution, which is a theory

Some scientists believe extinction is a normal part of evolution. Dinosaurs could not adapt to a changing environment. Is the spotted owl in the same position?

based on the rule of the survival of the fittest. According to the evolution theory, dinosaurs and woolly mammoths became extinct because they could not adapt to their changing environment. More adaptable species, such as squirrels and cockroaches, manage to thrive even in city landscapes. Evolutionists say that while humans happen to be dominant now, we may be replaced in millennia to come if we can't adjust to changing conditions on earth. These thinkers believe that it is unnatural to make a special effort to save a weaker species.[5]

Conservationists reply that the kind of extinction taking place now is anything but natural. Before humans arrived on the scene, species became extinct at the rate of about one per year. Now the rate is approximately 1,000 per year. In addition, the natural environment used to allow new life forms to emerge. Now new species that do manage to emerge often face great obstacles to survival.[6]

Conservationists have another unlikely foe: extreme animal rights groups. In California, animal rights activists tried to institute a moratorium (a waiting period) on hunting such waterfowl as ducks and geese. Conservation groups like the National Audubon Society joined hunters in a stand against the moratorium. Over 60 percent of California's wetlands is owned and managed by hunting groups. Hunters, like conservationists, have an interest in seeing the birds survive, because without them, their sport would be eliminated.[7] A moratorium could mean the loss of the hunters' support and thus the possible loss of the wetlands where the birds thrive.

CAN INDUSTRIES AND ANIMALS COEXIST?
Industry has provided the human race with many products, conveniences, and life-style choices. Factories supply us

Logging provides jobs and many products for homes and businesses.

with items such as clothing, packaged food, appliances, and cars. As the human population increases, industries expand to meet its needs. Are we willing to cut back our consumption of certain products if their production means the destruction of an animal species? How important to us, for example, is the spotted owl, when its survival might mean the loss of jobs?

Alaskans faced a similar dilemma in the 1970s, when vast supplies of oil and natural gas were found under Alaska's North Slope. Oil companies proposed building an 800-mile pipeline from the North Slope to the port of Valdez in Prince William Sound. Environmentalists opposed the pipeline at first, but the oil companies pledged that they would make every effort to protect the environment. The plan was approved and carried out.

For the next 15 years, Alaskans profited greatly from the oil industry. The state made so much money that residents no longer needed to pay income tax. In fact, state revenues generated from the oil industry were so great that residents received approximately $800 each year from the state. Existing businesses flourished, and many new jobs were created. New housing, schools, and highways were built with money derived from the pipeline, and no major environmental accidents occurred.[8]

Then on March 24, 1990, Alaskans awoke to the news of a huge oil spill. The oil tanker *Exxon Valdez* had crashed into Bligh Reef in Prince William Sound, and 11 million gallons of oil spilled into the water.

During the next few months, people worked day and night in an attempt to save animals—birds, seals, fish, and other marine animals—and clean up the mess. Eighty-eight species were affected. Biologists estimated that between

100,000 and 350,000 birds died from the oil; among them were 150 adult eagles. No one is sure how many other animals died. Biologists say that it may take 50 to 70 years for the animal population to return to normal.[9] In this case, the efforts of industry to preserve the integrity of the environment did not succeed.

WEIGHING THE COSTS AND BENEFITS

The presence of industry in an area often means acid rain, pollution, and the loss of plants, trees, and wetlands. When those conditions develop, entire species can become extinct. Some scientists estimate that if industry is allowed to go unchecked, we may lose 100 species per day by the year 2000.[10] But the earth's human population is growing and its needs are increasing. Industry means more homes, jobs, food, and cars. Under these circumstances, is it likely that humans will give animals equal consideration? Is there a way to balance development for human benefits with the well-being of animals?

Under the leadership of former vice president Dan Quayle, the U.S. government established a committee called the Council on Competitiveness. The purpose of this committee, nicknamed the "God Squad," was to allow businesses to bypass environmental regulations without getting the consent of Congress. According to one article, the committee "decide[d] whether saving jobs is more important than saving owls—in effect, whether some economic activities of humans are more important than the survival of a species."[11] The committee almost always put human economic activities first. Shortly after President Bill Clinton was inaugurated, he abolished the council.

The Society for the Prevention of Cruelty to Animals sponsors a dog walk in New York.

WHAT'S HAPPENING NOW?

In some ways, animal rights activists would like to fundamentally change the culture of American society. What we eat, what we wear, and how we look at ourselves in relation to the environment are at issue. What can we expect in the years to come? Animal rights groups such as PETA will probably continue to organize demonstrations and advertising campaigns against those whom they consider to be violators of animal rights. PETA plans to use consumer support to persuade industries to operate in a "cruelty free" manner. With the help of citizens, it hopes to push pro-animal laws through state and federal governments.

Members of the underground group ALF will—at least until they're caught—continue their raids and their liberation tactics. Although PETA has no official connection to ALF, it consistently publishes information received from ALF.

ANIMAL WELFARE GROUPS

More traditional animal welfare groups oppose ALF's tactics, but they are launching their own campaigns. "We don't think violence advances the cause of animal protection,"

The Humane Society of the United States is concerned about the overpopulation of unwanted animals.

said Dr. Martin Stephens, vice president in charge of laboratory animals at the Humane Society of the United States (HSUS). "It's true scientists are doing things to animals they wouldn't think of doing to people," he concedes. "But for now we think it's a justified and necessary evil."[1] HSUS and other humane societies are also attacking overpopulation, abuse, and other problems involving companion animals.

Humane and anti-cruelty societies see the issue of pet overpopulation as a priority in the 1990s. It is estimated that of the 70,000 kittens and puppies born in American homes, only 2 out of 10 will find good homes. Fifteen million stray or unwanted animals are destroyed in shelters each year. Ironically, many of these dead animals are ground into bone meal and used to make dog and cat food.[2]

The seriousness of the pet overpopulation problem was recently pounded home by the Peninsula Humane Society in San Mateo County, California. The society published an ad showing three large barrels of dead animals that had been gassed at the local shelter. The headline read, "And we couldn't do it without you." The result was a six-month moratorium on pet breeding in San Mateo County. Violators could be fined up to $500.[3]

Many humane societies are now offering low-cost spaying or neutering of animals before they can be adopted. Some require people to sign an agreement to spay or neuter pets before they can be adopted. Other humane societies conduct in-depth interviews with those interested in adopting an animal to educate them about the serious responsibilities of owning a companion animal. These programs appear to be working. Cities such as Los Angeles and Santa Barbara report significant reductions in the number of animals destroyed each year.

THE GROWING OPPOSITION

Meanwhile, opponents of animal rights groups have been mounting their own campaigns. Former U.S. Secretary of Health and Human Services Louis Sullivan and former Surgeon General C. Everett Koop have both made strong statements in support of using animals in medical research. Former Congressman Vin Weber of Minnesota organized the Congressional Animal Welfare Caucus. The primary purpose of the caucus is to support the role animals play in research. Former Secretary of the Interior Manuel Lujan publicly praised the role of hunters in managing wildlife.

In addition, the American Medical Association (AMA) has formulated the Animal Research Plan. Released in June 1989, the plan calls the actions of extreme animal rights groups "anti-science." It describes the activists as violent, responsible for illegal acts, and a threat to public choice. The plan's purpose is to promote the use of animals in research as humanitarian and worthwhile.[4] Organizations such as iiFAR and the Foundation for Biomedical Research have started active public relations campaigns. Both groups publish literature on the benefits of using animals in research.

People who had not been active in the animal rights debate are getting into the act. Kathleen Marquardt of Washington, D.C., was shocked that animals were being put on equal ground with people. In response, she started a group called Putting People First (PPF). This grass-roots organization has about 2,000 members in 16 states and is growing daily. PPF members can often be seen presenting their view of the issue at animal rights demonstrations.

CHANGING LAWS

Groups on both sides of the animal rights controversy have used and continue to use Congress, state and local legislatures, and the courts to win ground. Both sides have had some important successes and failures.

Researchers were disheartened when Congress defeated the 1990 Animal Research Facility Protection Act. Passage of the act would have made it a federal crime for anyone to steal animals from a research facility. If stealing animals had become a federal crime, the FBI could have been called to investigate the case.

On the other hand, a Texas court awarded the University of California in Irvine custody of four kinkajous that had been allegedly stolen from a researcher and housed by a group called Primarily Primates. The court ruling marked the first time a research institution had legally recovered its animals from the group that had allegedly stolen them.[5]

Animal rights activists lobbied hard for an amendment to the Animal Welfare Act that would have helped protect animals in the hands of unscrupulous animal dealers. But the amendment failed to pass in Congress. The Dolphin Consumer Protection Act did pass, however. It established the standard of using the words "Dolphin Safe" on tuna cans. These words will signify that the tuna were not caught in driftnets. Consumers can now support fishing companies that use dolphin-safe methods to catch tuna and boycott those that don't.

WHAT ARE THE CHANCES FOR CHANGE?
Think of all the world's problems in the 1990s—unrest in the Middle East and in the Commonwealth of Independent Republics, and perilous economic problems in many parts of the world, as well as in the United States. A skeptic might say that in such a stressful political climate, the plight of animals will be forgotten. In a world of limited resources, many people may think that the human suffering caused by war, poverty, hunger, and homelessness should take precedence over concern for animals.

Animal rights activists, on the other hand, suggest that there could be no better time than the present to examine our values and our position in the world in relation to all living things. Perhaps, they say, people will use the crises in the modern world as an opportunity for change—change in which animals will take their rightful place in the natural scheme.

Resources to Contact

AGRICULTURAL ORGANIZATIONS

Animal Industry Foundation
1501 Wilson Blvd., Suite 1100
Arlington, VA 22209

Farm Animal Reform Movement
P.O. Box 70123
Washington, DC 20088

The Humane Farming Association
1550 California St., Suite 6
San Francisco, CA 94109

National Cattlemen's Association
5420 S. Quebec St.
P.O. Box 3469
Englewood, CO 80155

National Livestock and Meat Board
444 N. Michigan Ave.
Chicago, IL 60611

ANIMAL RIGHTS ORGANIZATIONS

People for the Ethical Treatment of
Animals (PETA)
P.O. Box 42516
Washington, DC 20015

Trans-Species Unlimited
P.O. Box 1553
Williamspott, PA 17703

ANIMAL WELFARE ORGANIZATIONS

American Society for the Prevention of
Cruelty to Animals
441 East 92nd St.
New York, NY 10128

The Humane Society of the United States
2100 L St. N.W.
Washington, DC 20037

CONGRESS

The Hon. _____
United States Senate
Washington, DC 20510

The Hon. _____
House of Representatives
Washington, DC 20515

GUN AND HUNTING ORGANIZATIONS

International Shooting and
Hunting Alliance
1825 K St. N.W.
Suite 901
Washington DC 20006

National Rifle Association
1600 Rhode Island Ave. N.W.
Washington, DC 20036

ORGANIZATIONS FOR LEGAL ISSUES

Animal Legal Defense Fund
1363 Lincoln Ave.
San Rafael, CA 94901

Society for Animal Protective Legislation
P.O. Box 3719, Georgetown Station
Washington, DC 20007

ORGANIZATIONS THAT SUPPORT THE USE OF ANIMALS IN RESEARCH

California Biomedical Research
Organization
48 Shattuck Square
Box 114
Berkeley, CA 94794

Foundation for Biomedical Research
818 Connecticut Ave., Suite 303
Washington, DC 20006

iiFAR—Incurably Ill for Animal Research
P.O. Box 1873
Bridgeview, IL 60455

Fur Information Council
655 15th St. N.W, Suite 320
Washington, DC 20005

National Trappers Association
207 W. Jefferson St.
Bloomington, IL
61701

ORGANIZATIONS THAT OPPOSE THE
USE OF ANIMALS IN RESEARCH

National Anti-Vivisection Society
53 West Jackson Blvd., Suite 1550
Chicago, IL 60604

Physicians' Committee for
  Responsible Medicine
P.O. Box 6322
Washington, DC 20015

ORGANIZATIONS THAT OPPOSE
THE USE OF FUR

Canadian Anti-Fur Alliance
Toronto Humane Society
11 River St.
Toronto, Ontario M5A 4C2
Canada

International Society for Animal Rights
421 South States St.
Clarks Summit, PA 18411

ORGANIZATIONS THAT SUPPORT
THE USE OF FUR

Furbearers Unlimited
P.O. Box 4129
Bloomington, IL 61701

Fur Farm Animal Welfare Coalition
405 Sibley St., Suite 120
St. Paul, MN 55101

101

Endnotes

CHAPTER 1. THE DEBATE

[1]Sharon M. Russell, "CFAAR Celebrates World Lab Animal Liberation Week—With an Iron Lung!" *Coalition for Animals & Animal Research Newsletter,* Summer/Fall 1990.

[2]"Two Sides in Animal Research Issue Clash at Berkeley," *Arizona Daily Star,* 25 April 1990.

[3]Jack Hitt, "Just Like Us," *Harper's,* August 1989, 50.

CHAPTER 2. THE QUESTION OF RIGHTS

[1]Peter Singer, *Animal Liberation* (New York: Avon Books, 1975), 196.

[2]Tom Regan, *The Case for Animal Rights* (Berkeley: University of California Press, 1983), 3.

[3]Singer, 209.

[4]Ibid., 211.

[5]Ibid.

[6]Ibid., 8.

[7]Ibid., 214.

[8]Ibid.

[9]Sy Montgomery, "Can Animals Talk?" *This World Magazine,* 26 August 1990, 16.

[10]Singer, 9.

[11]Ibid., 2.

[12]Katie McCabe, "Who Will Live, Who Will Die?" *The Washingtonian,* August 1986, 115.

CHAPTER 3. ANIMALS AND THE LAW

[1]Singer, 212, quoting E. S. Turner, *All Heaven in a Rage,* 127.

[2]Edward F. Dolan, *Animal Rights* (New York: Franklin Watts, 1986), 17.

[3]Ibid., 76.

[4]Peter Singer, *Animal Liberation* (New York: Random House, 1990), 152.

[5]Ibid., 76.

[6]*iiFARsighted Report,* April 1988, 67.

[7]"Overview and Legislative Update," *Mainstream,* Spring 1990.

[8]"ALDF Sues USDA," *Animals' Advocate,* Spring 1990, 1-6.

[9]Sue Carswell and Susan Reed, "Animal Passion," *People,* 18 January 1993, 35-39.

[10]John G. Hubbell, "The Animal Rights War on Medicine," *Reader's Digest,* June 1990, 66.

CHAPTER 4. ANIMALS AND MEDICAL RESEARCH

[1]Robert W. Leader and Dennis Stark, *Animals in Biomedical Research* (Chicago: University of Chicago Press, 1987), 470.

[2]California Biomedical Research Association, *Kidney Disease Research,* pamphlet.

[3]California Biomedical Research Association, *Cancer Research,* pamphlet.

[4]Dolan, 26-27.

[5]Foundation for Biomedical Research, *Animal Research for Animal Health,* pamphlet.

[6]Foundation for Biomedical Research, *Portraits of a Partnership for Life,* pamphlet.

[7]Carswell and Reed, 38.

[8]Peter Singer, "What's Your Verdict?" *PETA News*, March/April 1990, 4.

[9]"A Pictorial of Laboratory Animal Abuse," *The Animals' Voice*, November/December 1990, 8-14.

[10]Sandra Bressler, interviews with author, 13 November 1990 and 8 January 1991.

[11]Animal and Plant Health Inspection Service, Regulatory Enforcement and Animal Care, and U.S. Department of Agriculture, *Animal Welfare Enforcement, Fiscal Year 1988: Report of the Secretary of Agriculture to the President of the Senate and the Speaker of the House of Representatives* (Washington, D.C.: Government Printing Office, 18 November 1989).

[12]Foundation for Biomedical Research, *Who Cares about Laboratory Animals?* pamphlet.

[13]Anna Sequoia, *67 Ways to Save the Animals* (New York: HarperCollins, 1990), 80.

[14]Dolan, 38-39.

[15]Sequoia, 80.

[16]Jeffry P. Cohn, *The Beginnings: Laboratory and Animal Studies, From Test Tube to Patient. New Drug Development in the United States*, An FDA Consumer Special Report, January 1988, 9.

[17]Foundation for Biomedical Research, *Portraits*.

[18]Foundation for Biomedical Research, *The Use of Animals in Biomedical Research and Testing*, July 1986, 8.

[19]Cohn, 2.

CHAPTER 5. ANIMALS AND AGRICULTURE

[1]Madeline J. Nash, "The Beef Against Beef," *Time*, 20 April 1992, 76.

[2]"Big Stink in Beef Belt, *Time*, 19 July 1990, 51.

[3]*World Book Encyclopedia*, 1993 ed., s.v. "Farm and Farming."

[4]U.S. Department of Agriculture, Statistical Reporting Service, 1989.

[5]*Information Please Almanac*, 1991 ed., s.v. "Table: Livestock on Farms."

[6]*Academie American Encyclopedia*, 1989 ed., s.v. "Factory Farming."

[7]*Information Please Almanac*, 1991 ed., s.v. "Tables: Per Capita Consumptions of Principal Foods, and Exports of Leading Commodities."

[8]Humane Farming Association, *Consumer Alert: The Dangers of Factory Farming*, pamphlet.

[9]Ibid.

[10]Michael Fox, *Inhumane Society* (New York: St. Martin's Press, 1990), 27.

[11]Animal Industry Foundation, *Animal Agriculture: Myths and Facts*, pamphlet.

[12]Ibid.

[13]Ibid.

[14]Betsy Freese, "No Shortcut to Pig Welfare," *Successful Farming*, August 1990, 24.

[15]Jim Mason, "Down on the Factory Pharmacy," *The Animals' Agenda*, July/August 1990, 47.

[16]Humane Farming Association, *Consumer Alert*.

[17]Mason, 47.

[18]Nash, 76.

[19]Animal Industry Foundation, *Myths*.

[20]"What It Takes to Get a Steak," *Science News*, 5 March 1988, 153.

21Nash, 77.

22Ibid., quoting Jeremy Rifkin.

23Animal Industry Foundation, *Myths.*

24Nash, 77.

25Humane Farming Association, *Consumer Alert.*

26"Back Page: Edifying Facts," *Utne Reader,* 26 July 1989.

CHAPTER 6. ANIMALS IN THE FASHION AND COSMETICS INDUSTRIES

1*Encyclopedia Americana,* s.v. "Cosmetics."

2Ibid., s.v. "Fur Trade."

3Rachel Urquart, "Images," *Vogue,* November 1990, 230.

4Kevin Renskers, Director of Toxicology, Avon, Inc., interview with author, 17 June 1992.

5Urquart, 20.

6Renskers interview.

7Ibid.

8William Plummer, "Trendy Aspen Warms up for a Showdown in the Bitter Cold War over Furs," *People,* 29 January 1992, 40–41.

9Richard Conniff, "Fuzzy Wuzzy Thinking about Animal Rights," *Outdoor Life,* February 1991, 92.

10Sequoia, 16.

11Ibid.

12Ibid.

13Conniff, 97–98.

14William C. Symonds, "Letter from Northern Ontario: How the Trapper Is an Endangered Species," *Business Week,* 6 May 1992, 24A.

15Conniff, 92–93.

16Symonds, 24A.

*The Fur Information Council, the National Trappers Association, the Fur Farmers Animal Welfare Coalition, and the North American Fur Auction dispute the 70 million and 30 million figures, but none of these groups could provide alternative statistics to the editor.

CHAPTER 7. ANIMALS AS ENTERTAINERS

1Singer, 190.

2Michael Hiderle and Michael Neill, "Making Waves," *People,* 30 September 1990, 94.

3Debra Jordan, "Living Trophies," *The Animals' Voice,* 45.

4"Wilder Places for Wilder Things," *Newsweek,* 17 July 1992, 59.

5Ibid.

6Jordan, 45.

CHAPTER 8. ANIMALS AND INDUSTRY

1"Environment's Little Big Bird," *Time,* 16 April 1990, 21.

2Ted Gup, "Owl vs. Man," *Time,* 25 June 1990, 56.

3Ibid., 57.

[4]"No Peace for the Spotted Owl," *Time,* 9 July 1992, 63.

[5]Norman D. Levine, "Evolution and Extinction," *BioScience,* January 1989, 38.

[6]Norman Myers, "Extinction Rates Past and Present," *BioScience,* January 1989, 39.

[7]Maura Dolan, "The Bambi Constituency," *This World Magazine,* 13 January 1991.

[8]Art Davidson, *In the Wake of the Exxon Valdez* (San Francisco: Sierra Club Books, 1990), xiii.

[9]Ibid., 294.

[10]Myers, 39.

[11]Maisie McAdoo, "An Owl or a Job," *Scholastic Update,* 17 April 1992, 13.

CHAPTER 9. WHAT'S HAPPENING NOW?

[1]Carswell and Reed, 37.

[2]Sequoia, 3-5.

[3]Stanton Samuelson, "Ban on Pet Breeding Raises Howls in San Mateo County," *San Francisco Chronicle,* 18 November 1990.

[4]Animal Protection Institute of America, "Overview," *Mainstream,* Spring 1990.

[5]Cynthia M. Langley, "Several Scary Things Are Occurring...," *CFAAR Newsletter,* Summer/Fall 1990.

Glossary

animal liberators: persons who believe in freeing animals from use in research, etc., so they can live their lives naturally

captive breeding program: a program that breeds endangered species in a place other than their natural environment

carcinogenic: cancer-causing

conservationist: a person who believes in using natural resources wisely so that they may be enjoyed in the future by others

driftnets: nets, sometimes 50 miles long, used to snare tuna

endangered species: a species that may become extinct in a short period of time if protective measures are not taken

euthanize: to kill in a painless way for reasons of mercy

extinction: the disappearance of a species

factory farms: a term used to describe large-scale farming operations

Food and Drug Administration (FDA): a federal agency that oversees the testing and approval of drugs and food

National Institutes of Health (NIH): a federal agency that conducts and supports a broad range of biomedical research and provides funds for the training of research scientists

paralysis: loss of the ability to move

primates: members of an order of mammals that includes humans, monkeys, apes, and other related species

rational: having the ability to reason and understand

resolution: a formal statement of opinion or intent voted on by an official body or assembled group

salmonella: a one-celled organism that causes food poisoning

sentient: having the ability to feel

speciesism: the belief that human superiority justifies the use of other species for the benefit of humans

utilitarianism: a belief that the useful is good and that right conduct is determined by the usefulness of its consequences

United States Department of Agriculture (USDA): the federal department that oversees the welfare of animals under regulation by federal law

vaccine: a preparation of microorganisms that is administered to produce immunity to certain diseases

vivisection: the cutting of a live animal in order to study its biological functions

Bibliography

Animal Industry Foundation. *Animal Agriculture: Myths and Facts* (1988), pamphlet.

Animals' Legal Defense Fund. "ALDF Sues USDA." *Animals' Advocate,* Spring 1990.

Animal Liberation Front. *Against All Odds: Animal Liberation 1972-1986.* London: ACR, 1986.

Animal Protection Institute of America. "Harp Seals on Ice." *Mainstream,* Spring 1990.

Animal Protection Institute of America. "Overview and Legislative Update." *Mainstream,* Spring 1990.

Animal Protection Institute of America. "Reporting from Washington." *Mainstream,* Spring 1990.

Animal Rights Network. "Death Before Slaughter." *Animals' Agenda,* February 1989.

Animals and Plants Health Inspection Service, Regulatory Enforcement and Animal Care, and U.S. Department of Agriculture. *Animal Welfare Enforcement, Fiscal Year 1988: Report of the Secretary of Agriculture to the President of the Senate and Speaker of the House of Representatives.* Washington, D.C.: Government Printing Office, 1989.

Berreby, David. "A Bill of Rights for the Barnyard." *Savvy Woman,* February 1989.

Budiansky, Stephen. "The Ancient Contract." *U.S. News and World Report,* 20 March 1989.

Compassion for Animals Foundation. "Worker Exposes Inhumane Slaughter." *The Animals' Voice,* vol. 2, no. 5.

Conniff, Richard. "Fuzzy Wuzzy Thinking About Animal Rights." *Outdoor Life,* November 1990.

Cowley, Geoffry. "The Wisdom of Animals." *Newsweek,* 23 May 1988.

Davidson, Art. *In the Wake of the Exxon Valdez.* San Francisco: Sierra Club Books, 1990.

Dolan, Edward F. *Animal Rights.* New York: Franklin Watts, 1986.

Dolan, Maura. "The Bambi Constituency." *This World Magazine,* 13 January 1991.

"Environment's Little Big Bird." *Time,* 16 April 1990.

Foundation for Biomedical Research. *Portraits of a Partnership for Life: The Remarkable Story of Research, Animals, & Man.* Pamphlet.

Fox, Michael. *Inhumane Society: The American Way of Exploiting Animals.* New York: St. Martin's Press, 1990.

Gup, Ted. "Owl vs. Man." *Time,* 25 June 1990.

Hitt, Jack. "Just Like Us." *Harper's,* August 1989.

Horton, Larry. *The Use of Animals in Medical Research: A History of Anti-Vivisection.* Stanford, Cal.: Stanford University Press.

Hubbell, John G. "The Animal Rights War on Medicine." *Reader's Digest,* June 1990.

Humane Farming Association. "Supermarket Chain Removes Anemic Veal From All Stores." *Watchdog*, Fall 1989.

Humane Society of the United States. *Close Up Report.* September 1990.

Humane Society of the United States. "Federal Report." *HSUS News*, Winter 1991.

Incurably Ill for Animal Research (iiFAR). *How Can You Show Your Support?* Pamphlet.

Incurably Ill for Animal Research. "Regulating Animal Research." *iiFARsighted Report*, April 1988.

Jordan, Debra. "Living Trophies." *The Animals' Voice*, vol. 2, no. 5.

Kaufman, Les, and Kenneth Mallory. *The Last Extinction.* Cambridge: Massachusetts Institute of Technology Press, 1986.

Kaufman, Stephen. "How Useful Are Animal Models?" *The Animals' Agenda*, September 1990.

Langley, Cynthia M. "Several Scary Things Are Occurring..." *CFAAR Newsletter*, Summer/Fall 1990.

Leader, Robert W., and Dennis Stark. *Animals in Biomedical Research.* Chicago: University of Chicago Press, 1987.

Levine, Norman D. "Extinction and Evolution." *BioScience*, January 1989.

McCabe, Katie. "Who Will Live, Who Will Die?" *The Washingtonian*, August 1986.

Montgomery, Sy. "Can Animals Talk?" *This World Magazine*, 26 August 1990.

Morrison, Adrian R., and Dominick P. Purpura. "Washington Watch." *BioScience*, March 1990.

Myers, Norman. "Extinction Rate Past and Present." *BioScience*, January 1989.

Perry, Nancy. "Race for Their Lives." *The Animals' Voice*, vol. 2, no. 5.

Plummer, William. "Trendy Aspen Warms Up for a Showdown in the Bitter Cold War Over Furs." *People,* 29 January 1990.

Roach, Mary. "Don't Wok the Dog." *California Magazine*, January 1990.

Romans, John R. *The Meat We Eat.* Canville, Ill.: The Interstate Printers & Publishers, Inc., 1985.

Russell, Sharon M. "CFAAR Celebrates the World Lab Animal Liberation Week—With an Iron Lung!" *Coalition for Animals & Animal Research Newsletter*, Summer/Fall 1990.

Ryder, Richard. "The Winds of Change: An Historical Perspective on Animal Abuse and the Animal Rights Movement." *Animal Voice Magazine*, vol. 3, no. 1.

Sequoia, Anna. *67 Ways to Save the Animals.* New York: HarperCollins, 1990.

Singer, Peter. *Animal Liberation.* New York: Avon Books, 1975.

Singer, Peter. "What's Your Verdict?" *PETA News,* March/April 1990.

"Spotted Owl Still in Danger." *Time*, 2 June 1990.

"What It Takes to Get a Steak." *Science News*, 5 March 1988.

"Wilder Places for Wild Things." *Newsweek*, 17 July 1989.

111

Acknowledgments

Armour & Co., 63 (top); Karen Chernyaev, 30 (bottom); Humane Farming Association, 55, 58, 63 (bottom); © Richard B. Levine, 56 (bottom), 75 (top), 83, 90, 94; Library of Congress, 12, 15, 17, 19, 39, 80; Minneapolis Public Library and Information Center, 76, 86; National Cancer Institute, 40; National Library of Medicine, 6 (both); People for the Ethical Treatment of Animals, 8, 30 (top), 43, 44, 70 (both), 73, 74; © Frances M. Roberts, 9, 18, 26, 41 (both), 56 (top), 66, 72, 75 (bottom), 78, 82; Southwestern Radiological Health Laboratory, 46; UPI/Bettmann, 34, 35, 51, 85, 89; U.S. Department of Agriculture, 23, 52, 60, 64; USDA/APHIS, 22, 31, 48, 96; U.S. Food and Drug Administration, 36; Western Wood Products Association, 91.